PENGUIN BOOKS

PHILOSOPHY FOOTBALL

Mark Perryman co-founded *Philosophy Football*, the self-styled 'sporting outfitters of intellectual distinction', producers of the Albert Camus goalkeeper's top and an entire squad of similarly cerebral football shirts, complete with philosophical aphorisms, and the sartorial inspiration behind this book. When he's not occupying his seat in the upwardly mobile West Stand at White Hart Lane, Mark is a regular contributor to *When Saturday Comes*. He is the author of the Fabian Society report 'Football United: New Labour, the Task Force & the Future of the Game' and is also editor of *Altered States* and *The Blair Agenda*, two collections of essays on contemporary political theory. *Philosophy Football* is, however, the first book Mark has felt grown up enough to write himself.

Philosophy Football

ELEVEN GREAT THINKERS PLAY IT DEEP

Mark Perryman

PENGUIN BOOKS

PENGUIN BOOKS

Published by the Penguin Group
Penguin Books Ltd, 27 Wrights Lane, London W8 5TZ, England
Penguin Books USA Inc., 375 Hudson Street, New York, New York 10014, USA
Penguin Books Australia Ltd, Ringwood, Victoria, Australia
Penguin Books Canada Ltd, 10 Alcorn Avenue, Toronto, Ontario, Canada M4V 3B2
Penguin Books (NZ) Ltd, 182–190 Wairau Road, Auckland 10, New Zealand

Penguin Books Ltd, Registered Offices: Harmondsworth, Middlesex, England

Published in Penguin Books 1997
1 3 5 7 9 10 8 6 4 2

Set in Monotype Onyx and Monotype Times
Typeset by Rowland Phototypesetting Ltd, Bury St Edmunds, Suffolk
Printed in England by Clays Ltd, St Ives plc

Contents

Big Shouts

Philosophy Football was founded in December 1994, just in time to fill a few friends' Christmas stockings with an Albert Camus goalkeeper's shirt. Quicker than you can say, 'When was the last time Spurs won the league?', Danny Blanchflower, Jean Baudrillard, Bill Shankly and Antonio Gramsci were being added to the squad of T-shirts, and *Philosophy Football* were dubbing themselves 'sporting outfitters of intellectual distinction'.

Without Hugh Tisdale the entire enterprise would still be an inspired marketing concept locked away deep in the nether regions of my crazed mind. Hugh provides the artistic wizardry that turns the intellectual quotations into fashion statements that would grace any catwalk. The fact that while this book was being written my team, Spurs, finally stopped losing to Hugh's favourites, Aston Villa, has done wonders for our working relationship.

Pedro and Jill of Kentish Town's finest T-shirt printers, Fifth Column, are also vital to our cause. Their qualities run to rarely smudging a shirt and being generous enough with their credit control to allow us to survive Eric Cantona's wavering intellectual popularity.

All our quotes are studiously researched for their authenticity, so while my economism with the truth makes me a sure-fire bet for the next Tory cabinet (whenever that might be, hah!), I remain indebted to John O'Reilly, Geoff Andrews, Peter Martin, Ben Lyttleton, Simon Arbuthnot and Toby Staveley for the source material they so carefully provided and I have so wilfully abused. For any readers who have in their hands a fragment of thoughtful insight from the great, the good and Arsène Wenger then I'd love to hear from you. If your particular player is picked for *Philosophy Football* immortalization on a T-shirt, you get the very first shirt to keep. Write to me at PO Box 10684, London N15 6XA.

Whilst writing this almighty tome it was most useful to be able to call upon the lugholes of Charlie Connelly, Jon Mustafa, Konrad Caulkett, Jeremy Gilbert, Tim Bewes and Herbert Pimlott. The fact that you grinned, laughed and sighed in most of the right places kept my desk even more untidy than usual as I ploughed on furiously with my scribbling.

Stephen Parrott gave the entire project some early ideological cohesion courtesy of the Birkbeck College 'Football, Culture and Society' (no, I'm not kidding) evening classes.

Penguin's Publishing Director Tony Lacey has shown the kind of sympathy and understanding that puts most club chairmen to shame. It just goes to show that going to book launches can be worth it, as it was in the dark corners of Scribes West that I first buttonholed the man. David Watson sharpened up the prose with a ruthless efficiency that would impress any pre-season training session. The cash-filled brown paper bag is in the post.

Doug Cheeseman of *When Saturday Comes* played a blinder with the cover image, and from the same half-decent football magazine, Tim Bradford brought my words to life with his customary illustrative genius. Faces were put to my eclectic squad selection by the inspired picture-research work of Gráinne Kelly.

I looked to Spurs to provide me with inspiration, but

sadly, with an injury list Gerry Francis no doubt could write a book about, the glory days weren't exactly on the horizon during the 1996–97 season. Still, as the god-awful dirge that fuelled the biggest giant-killing act of the year put it, 'things can only get better'.

Lastly, but the first choice on my personal team-sheet, Anne Coddington. The provider of more love, support and feedback than a boy could ask for. The fact that she was also writing her own book on football makes her patience and all-round reliability all the more remarkable.

Manager's Notes

Musing over the miseries of another disappointing home performance by Spurs is enough to cast the most hard-bitten fan's critical faculties adrift. Such was the source of the inspiration for choosing Albert Camus as our first signing for the squad at *Philosophy Football*. Of course, as both Jean Baudrillard and Umberto Eco would want to remind me in the course of any pre-match ideological pep talk, the fact that Albert was in reality a footballer as well as a philosopher is scarcely relevant. The unreal and simulacra are all the rage amongst the dons of postmodernism, and with Wimbledon's penalty claims, faith in fakes would appear to have its adherents down at Selhurst Park too.

Dave Sexton and John Beck – appropriately enough then manager at Cambridge United – were among the first to be cited by none other than the magazine

Philosophy Now for the depth of their intellectual canon; while the art magazine *The Tate* reliably, but amazingly, informs us that back in the sixties the troublesome Gallic trio Jean Genet, Jacques Derrida and Louis Althusser were regulars on the Paris Saint Germain terraces, no doubt joining the wags with the 'Who ate all the croissants?' chants. From such reports of great thinkers *Philosophy Football* was born. Part fantasy, part reality, our single-minded ambition was to find out what the world's greatest thinkers thought of the beautiful game. Strange to tell, it was a doddle finding a first eleven of clever-dick aphorisms, and if we top the table in the best-seller charts then you'll soon discover we've got plenty more where these came from: Homer, Kirkegaard, Orwell, Hite, Greer, McLuhan, Bunyan, Wordsworth, Cézanne and Shostakovich are all coming up through the reserve-team ranks and early reports suggest they each in their different ways are showing signs that they've got a big career ahead of them.

Our first-team selection begins with Albert Camus and ends with Bob Marley, with the midfield in particular displaying a broad range of influences combining Taoism,

Marxism, logical positivism and gay liberation. The net-busting quotations attributed to each player are all genuine enough, though the tales of their derring-do on the pitch belong in an alternative continuum. The *X-Files* has nothing on our ability to hunt out the truth from the most unlikely of sources. The programme-collecting reader who hankers after all things ancient may be disappointed that, with the exception of our Far Eastern import, Sun Tzu, the line-up is so decidedly modern, with more than a smattering of the controversial postmodern too. It's not that we've anything against the Greeks, though their better days are long gone and their well-structured defences do have an alarming tendency to turn into crumbling ruins. Rather, we felt that with all that spear-throwing, discus-tossing and hackneyed choruses of 'the football season is a marathon not a sprint', they might prove to be more trouble than they're worth. Socrates certainly did tempt us – after all, he's turned out for Brazil on more than a few occasions – but we've got to be rational about these things, and when you've been around for more than two thousand years your better days are bound to be behind you.

The Greeks do have something to teach all managers, players and fans, though – namely, stoicism. A trait that goes down particularly well at Highbury apparently with that student of the succinct, Ian Wright, summing it up very neatly in the maxim: 'Arsenal? You've got to take the rough with the smooth. It's like love and hate, war and peace, all that bollocks.'

At the root of philosophy is the attempt to find the answer to what we are wont to chant when an unknown physical property enters the known universe of the hallowed turf: 'Oo are yer?' It is perhaps, then, not such a surprise that some of history's finest minds found themselves putting away quill, typewriter or word-processor at 4.45 on a Saturday afternoon to catch up with all the scores. The great historian of Western philosophy, Bertrand Russell, was just one of those bewitched by the twenty-two men who would kick a brown leather spherical object, explaining Aristotle's metaphysics thus: 'The men who play football would still exist even if they never played football.' Good to see John Motson isn't alone in stating the obvious.

Football helped Bertrand and his ilk to find their

feet in a world of change and so what could be more appropriate than to repay the compliment by providing this fine bunch of lads, and not forgetting one lone lass, with a slightly exaggerated sporting CV? After all, it was only all that deep-thinking that deprived them of the training and dedication that would surely have enabled them to fulfil their footballing potential.

Known as the academicals, it was once thought that our team's future lay solely with the Scottish lower divisions, but now we know better. No more away trips to Partick Thistle, Forfar Athletic and Ross County. Instead, we're asking them to do battle for the future of civilization. The shoddy sponsors' logos, the fashion-disaster-inducing properties of bri-nylon and the multi-weave monstrosity formerly known as your away kit have had the field to themselves for too long. The *Philosophy Football* team play to win in 100 per cent cotton, thank you very much. Classic players of intellectual distinction. This is their story.

Mark Perryman

SEPTEMBER 1997

How the Team Lines Up

1. Albert Camus (1913–1960)

Nobel-Prize-winning existentialist author of *The Fall* and *The Outsider*. Born in Algeria, as a journalist, he wrote for the French Resistance underground press during WW2, and emerged as one of the post-war period's most important cultural figures during the 1950s.

2. Simone de Beauvoir (1908–1986)

The mother of feminism, author of fiction, a four-volume autobiography and *The Second Sex*. She helped us to understand the way men write of themselves as subjects, women as objects.

3. Jean Baudrillard (1929–)

One of the pioneers of postmodernism. A provocative writer fixated by the media world, he once famously declared 'The Gulf War Did Not Happen'. Proclaims the end of everything from truth to society in his work.

4. William Shakespeare (1564–1616)

England's greatest-ever playwright. Author of numerous tragedies, comedies and historical plays, he could also pen the odd romantic sonnet too. Now more likely to be thought of as Kenneth Branagh's scriptwriter.

5. Friedrich Nietzsche (1844–1900)

A thinker who is considered dangerous by some, with his blurring of the differences between good and evil. Never one to shirk controversy, he also championed the role of strong individualism in political leadership.

6. Ludwig Wittgenstein (1889–1951)

Austrian who travelled widely before settling in Britain. A contemporary of Bertrand Russell, he broke with him as he brought linguistic analysis to the very centre of his philosophical works.

7. Oscar Wilde (1854–1900)

Wit, author and man-about-town. Pilloried by the establishment for his exotic life-style, he was eventually sent to prison for what he poignantly described as 'the love that dares not speak its name'.

8. Sun Tzu (*circa* 500 BC)

Ancient Chinese general and military strategist of hazy vintage. His *The Art of War* now sells mainly to smart-suited advertising executives and corporate personnel managers looking for a sense of purpose in their business.

9. Umberto Eco (1932–)

University professor and best-selling novelist. *The Name of the Rose* is a medieval detective story that enthralled readers everywhere it was translated. His academic work is principally concerned with semiotics, the language of signs.

10. Antonio Gramsci (1891–1937)

Heroic Italian Marxist who died a tragically early death at the hands of Mussolini's fascists. His prison notebooks were eventually published posthumously and proved enormously influential with their description of how political power operates.

11. Bob Marley (1945–1981)

Musician and devout Rastafarian, in many senses the founder of reggae. Toured the world for his music, yet always found time to do what he could to bring peace between the warring political parties that bedevilled his homeland, Jamaica.

Albert Camus

Racing Universitaire Algérois and Algeria
Number 1: Goalkeeper

'After many years in which the world has afforded me many experiences, what I know most surely in the long run about morality and obligations, I owe to football.'

ALBERT CAMUS, *France Football*, 1957

Wearing the goalkeeper's number one shirt, Albert Camus was both the first man and the last, the final line of defence. Standing alone, he was charged with the momentous responsibility of keeping the ball out of his net when all around him had failed. With the ball swerving, catching the odd rebound, bobbling across a furrowed end-of-season pitch, it would rarely come to Albert direct, often catching him unawares. This unpredictability was to teach him much about the sad vagaries of life.

Pushing hard to reach the summit of his particular position, Albert tussled with the necessities of keeping a clean sheet, an ambition that was at one and the same time devoid of content yet full of the promise of victory. Such was his lonesome life on the goal-line. He met the problem head-on, knowing that to concede was not a legitimate option. He had to progress beyond the fate of the dodgy 'keepers who could undermine the achievements of his ten outfield team-mates. Such was his absurd reasoning, carrying the weight of the collective will within his lone self.

With the play all happening far away in the opposition penalty area, Albert often found time to reflect and to indulge in a touch of generous banter with those witty souls in the stands who would wail, 'You're *meeeeeeeeerde*!' each time his mighty goal-kick failed to reach its destiny and instead rolled uselessly off for a throw-in. Or he might amuse himself doing those endless stretching exercises which the modern 'keeper likes to impress with but which leave the rest of us convinced he'd be better employed as a part-time body contortionist.

Occupied at the back, Albert knew all about resistance, punching the ball or plucking it out of the air. Using every part of his body as he fearlessly threw himself at the feet of some marauding giant of a centre-forward bearing down on his goal. His artistry and determination were an inspired antidote to the dull conformity of his defenders, who appeared incapable of keeping up with the play, leaving Albert to clear up the near-certain ignominy they were creating for themselves. Out of this turmoil Albert was to find his reason for existing. Back and forth along his line, arms reaching for the ball, this was a life of immediacy and action and split-second decisions.

It is no accident that the 'keeper wears the number one, for the best of them are extreme individualists. These are the players who with one deft move or careless error can make or break a team's season. Once they wore green woolly sweaters and flat caps to distinguish themselves from the pack; now they're lumbered with the dubious pleasures of fluorescent synthetic fibres, dressed up like a tube of Smarties with outrageously padded shoulders and the odd pair of tights. But still they celebrate their difference, self-righteous in the knowledge that it is only they who have the right to handle the ball. Of course some of them like to think they can play a bit too. Rushing from their precious space between the posts, they put in a tackle or dribble the ball forward as if they were a spare man at the back. And for those that really want to get above their station, they can always try the Peter Schmeichel option: careering forward for that last-minute corner in the forlorn hope that the ball might find its way to them and heroically they'll put away an unstoppable header. Instead, they invariably have to rush back like the clappers only to watch helplessly as the ball sails over their own goal-line.

Albert knew that his role was stark in its simplicity: to keep out that which desires to go past him. *No Pasaran*, 'they shall not pass', was the motto he adopted from the memories he carried with him of the civil war that wreaked such havoc in Spain's defence. What he aspired to was a negation, his success or failure depending on just how good a stopper he was. At times Albert would revolt against the absurdity of his position. Who could possibly blame him if his full-backs lacked the pace to contain those long-limbed wingers who would streak past them before putting in a cross that rocketed off a centre-forward's forehead, with Albert just grabbing handfuls of air as the ball billowed out the netting? Or what could he do if in one of those goalmouth scrambles some poor, sad team-mate lashed out at the loose ball and promptly prodded it over his own goal-line? Albert

tried not to feel the guilt, to remain unperturbed, but as the goals-against column mounted up, he would turn against himself.

Exiled to the bench after one particularly poor performance, Albert came to think of home games with a kind of despair. All he could do was trot up and down the touchline with the secret ambition that he might be called upon once more when his replacement proved to be even more hopeless in goal than himself. Hero and villain: the two sentiments coexist for the goalie with a dreadful complicity. The resignation of picking the ball out of the back of the net goes hand in hand with the glory of prevention, the tiniest dividing line destined to decide his fate.

With injuries ravaging the gaffer's squad, Albert was once more given his chance to prove himself between the posts. And in that first game back he was forced to face the apparent certainty of the penalty-kick. If he could stop the ball, surely destined for goal (Gareth Southgate, after all, was just a flicker in his mum's eye back then) this would put him up there with the goalkeeping greats – Banks, Yashin and Zoff. As he stood, motionless, everything would reel before his eyes. Concentration was all as he focused in on the ball and the man, his whole body nervously coiled like a steel spring. In a flash he had moved, and in that moment the entire balance of the game would be decided. The ball was safe in his hands, and each successive shot was to be the undoing of others, not Albert. The intensely individualized glory of the penalty-save made up in the most magnificent of ways for all those games when he had been forced to shoulder the blame for the hapless failings of others. Men like Martin Heidegger, who would rush down the right letting loose balls whose direction you could never be sure of, or Dostoevsky, who was possessed of great talent but was destined never to fulfil his potential, or Ernest Hemingway, who had seen better days and for whom now the bell was surely tolling. At the moment of defeat Albert had always felt a terrible sense of loss, and in the eyes of others he was often the one at fault. It was this humiliation that created in him a detachment, an ability to see himself from the outside, and in that solitude he lost the goalkeeper's fear of the penalty. He had found his belonging and at least he had a clean sheet.

But to keep his place Albert knew he couldn't afford to bask in old glories. Justice was an honourable abstraction that few fans or managers shared; one mistake and once more he'd be found lacking. But if he found himself in that sorry position he also knew that he couldn't afford the luxury of emotion – he'd have to bottle up all that disappointment inside as the insults rained in on

'Fromage!' Cloth-capped Albert tries vainly to raise a smile, but existentialism got to him early in life and a right moody so-and-so it made him.

him from every direction. He knew that to promise a clean sheet week in, week out, was unreal. For every gravity-defying leap that saved the day there was a time when he would be rooted to his spot as the ball trickled over the line. Unable to drift in and out of the game, Albert had to have a deep-seated passion for the absolute, to find the truth of the clean sheet's nothingness without which no victory will ever be possible.

Albert tried to come to terms with the defeats, but it was only when he came to see the futility of his own situation that everything fell into place. His happiness was not in his own hands. It wasn't right for the rest of the team to judge Albert, for every player had more than enough to do themselves. The saving of the game was a collective responsibility, he came to believe, not one to be carried by the individual alone. Liberated, Albert could at last begin to enjoy his football. He tried, that was all he could do, and if that wasn't enough, then so be it.

Sadly, things didn't quite work out like this after all. Albert was still being left to carry the Perrier bottle for the team's defeats and after one particularly poor performance he found himself transfer-listed. This was the moment of truth. His career had turned into a struggle to survive in first-team football. And it was in these extremes of circumstance that Albert knew he would find his final happiness. Unable to depend on his team-mates for support, he decided that it was the individual who would henceforth be the point of departure in measuring the contribution he could make to the game. It was his own happiness that would always be his goal. No stranger to misfortune, he was determined to arrest his fall. Plaguing the boss with his requests for another chance, Albert was in danger of becoming an outsider in his own dressing-room until finally an opportunity came his way. With the injury-list mounting, the coaching-staff had no alternative but to give the out-of-favour Albert back his place. Determined to succeed, Albert wasn't one to further the misery of the team, and so he committed himself to pacifying the home support with a performance that would restore their faith in his prodigiously gifted ability.

Sure in himself, Albert threw himself across the goal just like the old days and no ball was destined to get past him on this most special of returns. But there was one rubicon he wasn't going to cross for any man. The dull cynicism of the professional foul wasn't for him; to pull the legs away from a forward destined to score was to mix up your ends and means. Never red-carded, Albert had a disciplinary record second to none, and whatever it cost, he wasn't going to sacrifice this most proud of all his achievements. Sure enough, his morality was put to the test as, in the dying moments of the game, from the far horizon of the pitch, a slow, persistent build-up was coming Albert's way. Two against two, the defensive odds were just about level but once his opponent was clean through it was now just Albert on his own who could save the day. Spreading himself wide Albert tried to narrow the angle but he knew that this wasn't enough, the target was just too huge for anyone to miss. Yet still Albert couldn't countenance anything illegitimate. He had to make the judgement, was this a save he could pull off? He couldn't afford the time to think, he just had to do it. He recognized the profundity of the situation: succeed, and he'd be carried off the pitch on his team-mates' shoulders, the hero of the hour; fail, and he'd be sent straight back to the bench in disgrace. As he looked up to the ball as it soared past his palms, his universe was in that moment divested of the illusion of human capacity. He curved his back beyond endurance and changed direction in mid-air. Agonizingly, he edged closer and closer to the ball in milliseconds that seemed to the thoughtful Albert as if they would last an eternity.

And then, the ball was tipped over the crossbar by hands that it had seemed would never reach it. At the heart of a great save like this is something inhuman. Albert shared the beauty of this inhuman performance with the task of keeping out that which is destined to go in. It is a feeling that only those who are called upon to wear the number one shirt will ever experience.

Simone de Beauvoir

Paris Saint Germain and France
Number 2: Right-back

'The woman who stands forth in the world seeking goals acquires that magnificent possession, the absolute.'

SIMONE DE BEAUVOIR, *The Second Sex*

Though a natural choice for the number two shirt throughout her long and distinguished playing career, Simone de Beauvoir set out to show that players in her position didn't have to come second. A pioneer, Simone was determined her side would never submit but battle long and hard for points home and away.

Simone was all too aware that her players could on occasion be passive, existing only inside their own clearly demarcated spheres of responsibility out on the pitch and lacking the capacity to effect a change to the game's apparently inevitable result. To win she knew she had to capture some of the qualities of her opponents who were, to a man, active, creative and only too happy to take the initiative. In her book these were winning ways and it was an illusion that her side couldn't have their fair share of them.

For Simone there was nothing natural about her side's weakness. Instead, she argued that the solution to their predicament was in their own hands: they couldn't just wait on other teams' results to go in their favour. If only her team-mates would begin to believe in themselves, they could achieve the results they craved for. Spicing up her side, Simone was glad to welcome some useful additions to the squad. Susan Brownmiller was useful in defence – any goals she conceded would definitely be against her will. Betty Friedan had a certain mystique about her, and veteran Mary Wollstonecraft vindicated herself on the rights, and the wrongs, of their play.

Long before all this fresh talent joined her team, though, Simone was concerned that the side's play was unduly negative. Lacking any autonomy, the players were too restricted, incidental to the play that passed them by, too many defining themselves in relation to those that purported to be their superiors. In fact, those who came out on top only did so because sides like Simone's were too ready to be also-rans. There was nothing solid about her midfield, and nothing exciting about her forward line, which performed well at home but didn't travel well.

A duo at the heart of the defence, married to their different tasks, seemed to be the first answer to Simone's problems. Riveted together, the pair of them ruthlessly patrolled their half, but beneath the happy surface the division of labours proved to be completely lopsided, so that as fast as one moved forward, the other was forced to retreat backwards. One had the desire to win, sure enough, but the other was unhappy to be lumbered simply with the domestic duties of defending. Fairly soon Simone came to the conclusion that there was no obvious reason why she should be wedded to these conventions. Tied up at home and battered as they so often were, Simone knew she had to free up these pairings, share out their duties equally; swapping roles, they would each be expected to do their fair share of sweeping up at the back. The change would do them both good.

Though Simone played at the back herself she had no need for rings of steel, or gold, to keep her in her place. But still the bulk of the squad were too easily subordinated, too ready to accept the defensive cover their partners offered them. Simone demanded independence, complete control over team selection, the right to choose a team that would strike out for themselves, players who refused to accept roles that were imposed upon them. They had to learn to take their chances, and if they did, she argued, the whole side would benefit. Inspirational at the back, Simone started to play the ball forward, full of confidence.

A dutiful player, through force of circumstance Simone came to stay in her best position, attacking full-back, for all of her career. With her fast-breaking runs no side of hers would die an easy death at the hands of the big boys. Nor would her players be isolated, trapped in the home half and incapable of breaking out. A tough tackler, she had the blood of others on her hands. She believed that there was nothing romantic about defeat, and she was never angrier than when a very easy goal was conceded right at the death. As a player she emphasized the contribution each individual could make to the side. There were plenty who underestimated her players, so she set out patiently to build up their own confidence. A long-time advocate of five-a-side, she found that in small groups the players raised the consciousness of their own ability and she could see some movement off the ball emerging out of these humble beginnings.

Simone preached engagement, taking the game to the other side. This fitted in well with the spirit of fellow players of her generation. Jack Kerouac had taken his side on the road to beat any team they played; John Osborne got into trouble for looking back in anger as any easy goal was conceded; Colin Wilson was a good player to have in an outside position; while Kingsley Amis was a Lucky Jim of a centre-forward, tucking away those easy goal-line toe-pokes. These were players who, like Simone, were free spirits out on the park, flitting from position to position, but while Simone was willing enough to play alongside them herself, she wasn't having any of them in her team. Their freedom to play depended on having players like Simone behind the ball and she wasn't going to be the subject of their tactical manoeuvres any more. In previous seasons John Stuart Mill, a huge influence on those who played the ball down the centre, eschewing both left and right wings, had subjected Simone's side to his play, but again she was having none of this. Simone was determined, more than ever before, to pioneer a whole new way for her own side to play.

This was to be the making of her. No longer satisfied by the odd individual performance, she needed the entire side to come to terms with their ability to win. She burned her boats and all sorts of bodily accoutrements we're too polite to mention, and there were some who felt Simone would suffer from a loss of support. But, as they say on the Left Bank, *au contraire*: her players were liberated from the drudgery of the mid-table position they had become too easily accustomed to. No longer would they put their faith in exceptional individuals who made no meaningful contribution to the system Simone was trying to put in place. Nor would she be satisfied with late token goals that just made heavy defeats look respectable. For Simone it was time for her side to get on top for a change.

She teamed up with her long-time playing partner, Jean-Paul Sartre, to try to turn things round. Jean-Paul

had suffered the ignominy of defeat himself. His trophy room was empty, just being and nothingness, no silverware to polish. Simone was never sure just how much she owed to Jean-Paul but her fans were certain enough that, in their all-black kits, this was a winning combination. Never one for conventional line-ups, Simone and Jean-Paul occasionally added a third player to turn the central midfield into a battling defensive triangle, full of passion, commitment and two-on-one situations.

With Jean-Paul at her side, Simone shook the rest of the team up. Making space for themselves, they began to understand the roles they could play. There was nothing predetermined about their lowly position. They knew they could climb the table: it was only bad faith that had kept them out of a top-ten end-of-season place. Poor Sigmund Freud drove himself crazy with envy as Simone's side soared up the league.

With her home form sorted, the question of penetration needed to be settled if Simone was to see her side putting away enough goals. Friedrich Engels seemed to think that he had got to the origin of the problem, but many remained dissatisfied with his economic distribution of the ball. Simone knew that for long periods her undoubtedly gifted side let the other side dominate. It was something certainly to do with the way their opponents structured their formation, keeping Simone's side off the ball. Deprived of possession, Simone was determined to play her way back into the game. Turning the game around, she broke rules, did as she liked and got her players to assert themselves. This was to be no one-sided contest, and when a second wave of players similarly committed to changing the system joined the squad, she knew things were at last moving her way.

By the end of Simone's playing days the physical side of the game was no longer an issue, with players going into their labours as and when they wished. Sigmund Freud had only got it half right when he said the game was all about the tackle. Simone was to prove that the whole game really was made up of two halves, and that her players had as much right to be in one half as the other. Crashing the ball through the stadium's glass ceiling, this was a side that was doing it for themselves. Indiscriminate with the ball, they spread it far and wide – they weren't going to be closed down by anyone. At last this was a team that was neither trapped at home nor unable to get a result away from home. Simone knew other teams would no longer be doing the double over her, and should they try she always knew that, with Lorena Bobbitt up front in an attacking position, she had the player to cut them off in their prime.

Jean Baudrillard

Paris Saint Germain and France
Number 3: Left-back

'Power is only too happy to make football bear a facile responsibility, even to take upon itself the diabolical responsibility for stupefying the masses.'

JEAN BAUDRILLARD, *In the Shadow of the Silent Majorities*

"Power is
only too
happy to

The proverbial *enfant terrible* of any classical defence, Jean Baudrillard was always better on the attack than defending his position. He accused the centre of collapsing as his fellow defenders became fragmented, losing touch with reality and drifting out of the game. Feeding the ball forward, Jean preferred passes that skimmed across the playing-surface, while encouraging his back four to move up the pitch again and again, rejecting calls to play deep. He was out to break up the rigid formalities of four-four-two that the more traditionally minded tried to impose on their players and was one of the first to propose the free-floating 'three at the back', transforming the wearisome back-pedalling full-back into a swashbuckling attacking wing-back darting back and forth the length of the pitch.

But Jean didn't just change how he lined up his side

to give a new shape to their game. He could play a bit himself too. He was the master of the dummy, shimmying this way and that. You never quite knew who the ball might go to or where it might end up, and best of all he loved to nutmeg, poking the ball through the big bruiser of a centre-half who, in the pre-match build-up, had gruffly promised to give out the 'ard stuff to the delicate Jean. In the early part of his career Baudrillard played the dummy as simply a fake ball: looking up the pitch, he acted as if he was about to hoof it, the opposition ran to mark the centre-forward, and then Jean mischievously passed the ball out to the wing and the break was on. Soon enough, with the renaissance of flair football that Jean himself epitomized, others caught on and every defender was copying the inimitable Baudrillard dummy. Times had changed, and managers had started to drill their innocent charges in the whys and wherefores of modern football. Now the dummy became simply a means of missing out one of the back four as the game went across the pitch, all sideways and skyways rather than the dazzling dribble and tactical trickery that the young Jean had once dreamt of. The dummy was being mass-produced, devoid of the meaning that Baudrillard had previously bestowed upon it. And just when he thought it couldn't get any worse, it did. The post-match magic-marker pen and panels of summarizers were the death-knell of individual creativity. Night after night Andy Gray sketched out a model for the game in his video vault that managers followed in droves. Out came the blackboards, coded passwords and arms aloft to translate those carefully rehearsed training-pitch moves into drab execution. Models ruled the roost, each trick drilled then cloned through the first team, past the reserves down into the nether regions of the apprentices and schoolboy hopefuls whose results in the back of the programme supporters would dreamily drool over.

With every half-decent team copying the moves of their wealthier betters, football pretty soon looked the same from park-side to Premier elite. Jean lofted the ball into hyperreality in sheer frustration: the only thing that was real any more was what could be copied. A passing commercial manager's ears pricked up. Rubbing his sweaty palms, he headed down to some fly-by-night backstreet factory to start churning out replica kits by

the barrow-load. Suddenly you weren't little Joe Brown racing down the wing for the Cub Scout First Eleven, but David Beckham, well, at least according to the name and squad number on your back. And all those long-named East European imports were a financial godsend at £1 a letter. Sadly though, as West Ham were soon to discover, the profitability of the lettering service was meagre compensation for the unpronounceable stars' glaring inability to perform out on the pitch.

With his two full-backs now performing midfield duties, the gaps in the defence were more than made up for by Jean's massed midfield. Jean, like that other great left-back, Karl Marx, remained concerned that, when push comes to shove, all that was solid in the middle of the park might melt into air. The midfield were supposed to pick up the ball, soak up any attack and explode into action with a quick break that caught the opposition unawares. Too often, though, they simply knocked the ball around, opening up a great big hole in which nothing ever happened except aimless short passes that went nowhere and time after time were pounced upon by a snapping-at-your-heels forward who then bore down on your defenceless 'keeper and put the ball away with ruthless efficiency. There were just too many gaps for his defenders to plug, his back three were engulfed and the team was staring relegation in the face. Too good to go down? It was a sentence that confusingly combined both reality and unreality, and the drop beckoned. And with the loss of their Premiership status the fans would be feeding their insatiable desire for Saturday afternoon spectacle elsewhere. The glory, glory days would be no more. Jean massed his five-man midfield together for one of those vital six-pointers which might determine his side's fate – not that Jean had much faith in determinism, nor fate for that matter, but that's by the philosophical way. A bit of positive brutality was called for, no more belly-up surrendering of the midfield in the face of some star-studded forward line that reckoned a hat-trick was theirs for the asking. Getting his retaliation in first, Jean grabbed a goal and put an end to the critics who said there was no substance to his game and that he was incapable of winning a point, let alone three.

This being an away match, Jean's team bade a none-too-fond farewell to the home team's masses, who, wrapped up in their after-match misery, stole away from the stadium in stony silence. Gone were those table-topping dreams that the tabloid tipsters had promised them that very morning. Oh, the vicissitudes of time, motion and a lucky goal in three. Casting a shadow of gloom over the joy of the travelling support, the home fans had nothing to say, trying to deny the humiliation of the lost three points and secure in the knowledge that Jean's team were still a bunch of has-beens and never-will-bes with those long trips to Grimsby and Darlington still firmly on their horizon.

But the win was in the bag, and for at least the next twenty-four hours his critics got off Jean's back. Never one to settle, by Monday Jean was once again putting his midfield through their paces down at the training ground. More conscious than most of his side's defensive frailties, Jean was mindful of those who urged him to sign a tough-tackling ball-winner to give some backbone to the team. But Jean wasn't to be persuaded that such strong-arm tactics would suit the balance of his team. In their place Jean preached the strategy of seduction, coaxing the ball out of the tackle rather than kicking your way to possession. The very mention of seduction was enough to get his testosterone-overdosing charges' libidos into gear and for the next twenty minutes at least he had their undivided attention. The secret, Jean explained, was to appear hard as nails, not necessarily to be so. So the ghetto-blaster on full in the changing rooms, beating your head against the tunnel wall –

number one crops were to be tonsorially *de rigueur* (Jean liked to slip those continental *bon mots* into his coaching sessions) – and plenty of expletive-ridden 'avin a word with the ref should do the trick. As the team lined up that Saturday, full of confidence with those new tactics drilled into them, many of the crowd were shocked to see their former favourite Michel Foucault dropped. Jean was exasperated: forget Foucault, he doesn't understand the exercise of power out on the pitch, he structures his play all wrong, and he doesn't fit in. Soon enough, the once mercurial Foucault was being transfer-listed, destined to go back to where Baudrillard was convinced he truly belonged, in the lower divisions. Meanwhile, back out on the pitch, the ball was being seduced back onside but the result could still go either way, with the opposition catching on and playing Baudrillard at his own game. Fortunately the whistle did eventually blow; with each side cancelling the other out a 0–0 draw was the only likely outcome, however long they played. The two sides simply couldn't be separated, so a point apiece seemed just about fair.

With Foucault now out of the side, Jean was looking

for some new signings. Jacques Derrida certainly appealed: he weaved his way across the park, teasing his opponents as he let them catch sight of the ball before turning on a sixpence, having deconstructed their defences. His 25-yard volleys, which he lashed goalwards with bewildering accuracy, suggested he would fit perfectly into any team run by Baudrillard. But the Canadian media-darling McLuhan was another player that Jean liked the look of, and he could be sure that McLuhan would always get the messages that Jean passed out to the players from his position at the back, whatever the medium – 'ollering, or arms waving.

Jean knew that the team didn't have much strength in depth, but that had never worried him before. Up his sleeve Jean had one remaining fatal strategy to save the side's season. Evil wasn't the word for it. Jean's side contested every decision, and certain goals were disallowed as the referees wilted under the storm of protest that Jean unleashed. Truth went out of the window, with dives earning penalties and accidental handballs emerging from nowhere to keep Jean's side in matches they would otherwise have surely lost. However much the other lot complained, and never mind the endless action-replays showing just how wrong the ref was, the result still stood, and come the end of the season Jean's team were still there to fight another day.

But for Jean their final league placing hardly mattered. They'd escaped the drop but their position was just an illusion. Jean realized there wasn't any future for him at the club. The team would always be there or thereabouts but the early-season dream of winning one of the cups was now just a far-away memory, cooled off and dusted down by the lack of objects in the trophy room. Robbed of success? If only Jean could solve this most perfect of crimes. He could hit the post but the bulging net defeated him, and so the final victory would never be his. Hanging up his boots, he knew it was time to move on, though he knew not where, he never did.

William Shakespeare

Aston Villa and Merrie England
Number 4: Play-maker

'Am I so round with you as you with me
That like a football you do spurn me thus?
You spurn me hence and he will spurn me hither
If I last in this service you must case me in leather.'

WILLIAM SHAKESPEARE, *The Comedy of Errors*

Midlands play-maker William Shakespeare loved to bring the ball forward from where it was stalled at the back through to the centre circle so that he could dictate the play. Measure for measure, Will was a match for anyone, a tempestuous tackler who darted back and forth ensuring that his passes were delivered into the box. And when there was a breach in the defence against a marauding French forward line, everyone knew that Will could be counted on once more. With Will snatching the win thanks to his goalmouth heroics, there were plenty who would agree that all's well that ends well.

Well-travelled, the whole world was Will's footballing stage. Greece was one stop on his continental career, and in his book the Mediterranean was definitely the place to prosper, particularly if one could master the aerial game. Making his way to Italy, two gentlemen of

Verona persuaded Will to join their newly promoted club in the Serie A and it was here that he was able to build a team around him of his own making.

In the middle of defence Will placed the doomed partnership of Mark Antony and Cleopatra. Mark had recently masterminded the defeat of those south coast sleeping giants of the English league, Pompey, but playing alongside the sultry Egyptian temptress Cleopatra he only had eyes for her, rather than the ball. The pair of them were doomed from the start; their game went to pieces as legion after legion of forwards descended on their penalty area. As if his lack of concentration wasn't bad enough, Mark saw the elder statesman of the side, Julius Caesar, stabbed in the back by the vicious hard-tackler in the toga, Brutus. Forced into changing the squad numbers around, with Caesar stretchered off by a couple of intinerant pall-bearers, Will hastily threw Brutus his new shirt with the destined-to-be-immortal words: 'You Two, Brutus'. Meanwhile Mark Antony rallied his troops for one more attempt to shore up the defence. He called for every man, and in Cleopatra's case woman, to give their all, 100 per cent commitment

and all that barn-storming guff you get when you're 2–1 down, one point adrift from safety and relegation is staring you in the face with five minutes to go in the last match of the season. It wasn't to be, though. Mark Antony was a tragedy waiting to happen, with his strength sapped by too many eve-of-match, late-night liaisons courtesy of Cleopatra. The team surrendered their slender half-time lead with Cleopatra failing in her bid to snake her way upfield. Her tasty bit of dribbling across her own box had gone all suicidal when she lost the ball just six yards out and an easy goal was slotted home to send the side down.

Realizing that any day now his run would be coming to an end, Will met up with a merchant of Venice in some dodgy-looking pizza parlour next to one of those roads the Romans were so good at building. Shylock was his name. A bit of a tight so-and-so, he agreed to take Will on loan. There wasn't even an under-the-table bung, but if Will didn't score a hatful of goals Shylock would be wanting his pound of flesh. The curtain-raiser to the season duly came and Will's new club, Venezia, were predictably sunk without trace. Straightaway Shylock was on poor Will's back and a nasty court case soon ensued. Will was happy enough to give up his pound of flesh but when Shylock overstepped the mark and demanded blood, guts and all sorts of other bodily bits and pieces, Will's doughty defence lawyer successfully proved the contract to be null and void. As they celebrated on the court steps, the photo-opportunity turned into a tabloid sensation when the hero of the hour, Will's brief, turned out to be not so much a hero as a heroine. Will was a liberated sort of chap, though, and he was all for a bit of swapping around to mix up his side's roles.

But, time waits for no man, so, despite his many seasons in Italy, Will was ready to move clubs once again. He'd heard something was rotten in the state of Denmark's defence – after all, John Jensen was one of their star players and Danish agents were even more unscrupulous than Shylock with their offloading of Scandinavian ne'er-do-wells on many an unsuspecting English club side looking for a bit of European glamour. Denmark proved not to be the dream move Will had hoped for, though he did discover he had the ability to steal a scene as well as anyone. Will was by this time a mean talent-spotter and when he plucked the moodily precocious young Hamlet from his lonely spot on the terraces of small-time club, Elsinore, he knew that he was on to someone who really would make the big time. No slacker at the back, Hamlet ghosted his way past defenders, dispatching old-timers who tried to screen the ball from him like there was no tomorrow. Up front it would all be 'Frailty, thy name is Woman', as he'd contemptuously cry out when another girl's-blouse-of-a-waspish-forward suffered at his boots, or 'Get thee to a nunnery', if he thought his own lot were being a bit too tentative in the tackle. He'd no need for slings and arrows either as he took on his opponents and beat them. Hamlet's part of the pitch was like a graveyard, with forwards picking themselves off the floor and ruing the day they'd crossed his path.

There was to be no happy ending to Will's stay in Denmark. Hamlet proved to be another one of those promising youngsters with a fatal flaw. Murder, drugs, girlfriend who drowns herself and a dad who's been topped by his brother, who then marries the poor dead lad's wife, were more than enough to wreck any career. When it came to the crunch, no big club would take him on. To the question 'To be or not to be', poor Hamlet got a resounding thumbs down.

Will headed back home to try his luck in the English league. His first foray was with King Lear's outfit, who played a zonal defence system, dividing their half into

Pit bull terrier makes first menacing appearance on park touchline. Note swords thrown down to make goal.

three parts. They constantly squabbled and the ball kept coming between them, driving the players mad. Playing in all conditions, this was no joyful homecoming for Will, who'd become accustomed to sunnier climes, and in torrential rain coupled with blustery winds he found it difficult to keep control of the slippery ball. The three at the back just didn't work out and it was only with the timely arrival of some French reinforcements to their depleted squad that Lear found a way out of the futile tactics that had blinded his ambition.

Will was out on his ear. Though the weather was scarcely likely to be any better than old Lear's storms, Will thought he'd like a run-out with a Scottish outfit. Teaming up with Macbeth and his sometime ally, Macduff, Will was soon enough laying on goals aplenty for the pair of them. But the early promise of success was to end in tragedy with a fearsome penalty shoot-out. The tried and trusted three-man defence had bewitched their opponents for a while but when the crunch came and everything depended on slotting home from six yards all Will could mutter was, 'Out, damned spot-kick', as the ball sailed over the bar into the heather and mist. With his career north of the border ending in a right old blood-letting at the club, this part of the story is so associated with misery and being murdered by lesser sides that Will refuses to refer to it by name.

Back in England, Will had heard that a merry time would be had if he joined up with his old mate Falstaff at non-league hopefuls Windsor. Falstaff was known to be a bit of a lad, and soon there were all sorts of tales of mistresses, wife-swapping and high jinks. Run out of the club, Will and Falstaff were offloaded to Shrewsbury Town and they really thought their luck was in when Shrewsbury drew London's famous Hotspurs in the cup. But this was not to be their day. They battled hard enough but at the back Will just couldn't put on a show like the old days and his play, though full of character, was a comedy of errors.

There was no alternative but to head back to Europe. It was back to the Gianfrancos, Fabrizios and Paolos of yesteryear in the Italian league. An early champion of the African game, on his return to Venezia Will brought in the dark and brooding Othello to shore up his defence. Othello was a tower of strength, but sadly he was let down by his none-too-trusty lieutenants. Courting tragedy, Othello became racked with jealousy and he smothered his chances of really making his mark. Once again Will had happened upon a player whose early promise met its match on the big stage.

Will didn't want to end his career on a sad note, though. He might have had his fair share of tragedy but he'd raised the odd laugh too, and parts of his play were certainly historic and would be reproduced many times over once he'd retired. Going back to where his Italian career had begun, Verona, Will decided to see out his playing days by settling the boardroom battles that were tearing the club apart. Two warring factions, the Montague and Capulet families, had built up their shareholdings to such a degree that only by settling their differences could the club be saved. Will brought in an unknown youngster, Romeo, who was a Montague but put his kit through the wrong washing programme in the launderette so no one could read the name on his shirt. Almost as soon as he first touched the ball the Capulet followers were being wooed by Romeo's deft moves on the park, and when he was on the bench they'd yell from high up in the executive boxes, 'Romeo, where art thou, Romeo?' (The Capulets were an educated mob and weren't too familiar with footballing colloquialisms.) One Capulet fan in particular had her fire all lit up by young Romeo. Juliet loved the way he played and he fair well swept her off her feet. She didn't even mind when she found out he was a Montague, so Verona United looked like a racing certainty when they secretly married away from the glare of the paparazzi and their zoom lenses. There are precious few happy endings to Will's tales, though, and this doomed pair just couldn't say no to drugs, potions and the like.

The curtain was down on Will's career. He was a man who created performances out of nothing and never lost the plot. The winters weren't just full of discontent: he could raise a cheer too as he turned in performances that saw his side winning those Boxing Day derby matches and breaking clear of the early season chasing pack by the time Twelfth Night came around. Will had proved himself to be the ultimate utility player, travelling far and in his time playing many parts.

Friedrich Nietzsche

FC Basel and Germany
Number 5: Central Defender

'The Formula of my Happiness: a Yes, a No, a straight line, a goal.'

FRIEDRICH NIETZSCHE, *Twilight of the Idols*

One of the game's original hard-men, Friedrich Nietzsche is a man of superhuman strength, lulling the opposition into a false sense of security with his shabby kit, socks down around his ankles and shirt flying in the wind. Hunchbacked and short-sighted, he's hardly physically equipped to strike fear into the opposing centre-forward. But unleash his anger, and from behind those deep-set eyes and that droopy moustache comes a raging torrent of physical commitment.

Friedrich's tough-tackling, no-nonsense approach to the game has got him into trouble more than once. Football's authorities have delighted at throwing the book at this upstart who has little or no time for rules that try to stop him charging this way and that, putting in those last-ditch tackles that invariably lead to a penalty. 'I went for the ball, the ball!' Friedrich would scowl as some effete lightweight writhed around in over-dramatic agony, only to pick himself up off the floor to put the ball away from the penalty spot a matter of seconds later. Friedrich would slope off the pitch, having been shown the obligatory red card, enduring his solitary sentence, shunned by his team-mates, who had to play on with the game slipping beyond their grip.

Dogged by disciplinary problems, he couldn't stay in one place for long. Nietzsche plied his trade across Europe, forsaking the Bundesliga of his homeland for French, Swiss and Italian teams. Long mistaken for one of those pumped-up internationals who beat their chests and click their boots together at the merest whiff of their national anthem, Friedrich actually preferred to shuffl nervously before kick-off, mumbling the words, embarrassed by all the pomp and circumstance.

His was a playing style of extremes. He wanted to push harder, run quicker, kick the ball faster than anyone else. Playing to the limit for Friedrich meant pushing out of the way those who obstructed his path forward. The shoulder-charge and flailing elbow were a vital part of his play, and if your anatomy connected with his,

didn't you just know it. Opponents would troop off the pitch, black and blue all over, while Friedrich proudly boasted that at least they knew they'd been in a game. Sentimentality and manners were never his strong points and his popularity plummeted as team after team suffered at his hands, legs, arms and boots. He was immune to calls for a bit of polite pussyfooting: he was on a mission, out to force football to change. Why did referees have to blow the whistle every time he stepped out of line? Play the advantage for once, let the physical side of the game flourish and the strongest teams will win the three points they deserve, while the weaker ones can fight it out at the bottom of the table.

Playing alongside Friedrich in the early part of his career was a player with an iron will to succeed. Bismarck united his team of many talents, though later he was to sink without trace and now he's probably running a pub somewhere, like many an ex-pro. It was, however, his coach Schopenhauer who taught Friedrich as an apprentice-footballer all he knew about defensive play, convincing him that football could be the making of a young fellow, taking your mind off the dreary drudgery of all those first-team players' boots you had to polish and the terraces that needed sweeping. The centre-half that Nietzsche was destined to become would be an all-powerful figure, breaking up attack after attack and always causing mayhem in the opposition box as he launched himself into the air to put away an unstoppable header.

Friedrich's football didn't start off in the happiest of

circumstances. His first season saw his side tragically relegated and his then happy-go-lucky manner was transformed. He became sour-faced and never looked a TV camera in the eye again. He stood tight-lipped and impassive as the taunts rang out all round the stadium: 'Down with the Hammers, you're going down with the Hammers'. The cruelty of being out there on the pitch was laid bare and Friedrich had to take it, all alone. There was only one way to banish the memory: the team had to come straight back up. And this they did. The tragedy was over, the team were a bunch of heroes where last season they'd been a bunch of losers; once again they were up there playing the game the way it should be, at the very highest level.

Much of this early success was down to the way Friedrich teamed up with new signing Richard Wagner. On the face of it, these two were ill-suited, but for a couple of seasons they played in harmony, and the results, so the manager of the time loudly proclaimed, were music to his ears. He must have been tone deaf then, because while Wagner was running rings round the odd defender, the rest of the side were no longer in tune with the direction he wanted to take them. Friedrich's patience finally snapped when Richard's bonkbusting bedtimes were revealed in a super soaraway exclusive.

Friedrich was having none of this decadent lifestyle. Turning his back on Wagner, he once more set out to build a side in his own image. He dallied with the newly formed partnership making hay down the left wing, Karl Marx and Friedrich Engels, but their determination to play a collective game, sharing out the responsibilities to tackle and score equally between all eleven players, hardly suited Nietzsche. He was all for man-to-man marking, he could play tight, but he was a born wanderer too. Karl was quick enough to appreciate this, but when he finally turned his back on Nietzsche he left him to his bitterest rivals, who ran down the right wing. They finally signed Nietzsche up when he was in the twilight of his career. Friedrich knew best though: he was his own man and, whoever's shirt he wore, his certainty in his own success always shone through.

He was a realist too. Playing his way up through the lower divisions never particularly worried him. He was sure enough of his own talent, though as the seasons went by and the scouts on the touchline eyeing up this tower of strength at the back became rarer and rarer, he did get a tad bitter and twisted. Manager after manager tried to instil their own ideas in this wonderfully gifted defender, but Friedrich was having none of it. He knew precisely how he wanted to play the game. In his book the science of football would always triumph over the artistry of the delicate passing game favoured by others. The illusion of victory was no good to Friedrich, he wanted to see those three points safely in the bag before he would let the side take their feet off the pedal. His team-mates' ears would still be ringing with Friedrich's tirelessly shouted stream of instructions long after the ninety minutes was up. Pity wasn't a word Friedrich was particularly familiar with as he bellowed at some match-scarred full-back panting with exhaustion but expected to play out of his skin right to the final whistle. There was no substitute for a ball struck squarely and Friedrich expected each and every one of his team-mates to strike that ball for all they were worth. He might be human, the proverbial bloke behind you might say, but he's more than human too.

When his side finally came to play in the Premiership and had the league leaders in their sights, Friedrich relished the idea of toppling the previous season's champions from their familiar top-of-the-table perch. And when the team did precisely that, Friedrich was the first to claim that this meant the champions weren't invincible – they could be beaten and they didn't have any god-given right to the championship.

But he couldn't shake off his reputation for toughness at the expense of skill, even after his side topped the table. Believing himself beyond good and evil, he courted yellow cards like there was no tomorrow. With the cautions mounting up, Friedrich was looking at a very long suspension. This was to be his downfall. Never to play a full season, his playing became more haphazard as each run of good games was broken by his enforced absence from the pitch, a situation exacerbated by Friedrich's near chronic susceptibility to injury. Hamstrings, groins, cruciate ligaments, Achilles' tendons and just about every other part of his body he'd sprained, strained and snapped with alarming regularity. It would drive him mad, though with his face gripped in an agonizing grimace he seemed to take a perverse pleasure in playing through these career-threatening injuries that would have felled a lesser man long before the stretcher took him reluctantly off to the sidelines.

Such was his will to win that Friedrich was a real handful to manage. Combative to the last, he'd be the first to set the crockery in mid-air motion if his side was losing at half-time. 'Is there such a thing as up and down any more?' Thus spoke his Greek team-mate Zarathustra, as one of these sessions started to turn particularly nasty. These foreign imports just didn't seem to understand three up and three down meant that if you were twenty-second out of twenty-two there was only one answer: the ignominy of relegation. Friedrich's game began to lose any meaning as the side surrendered its tenuous grip on mid-table survival, confirming his pessimistic pre-season prediction for the club's future. He lashed out in every direction, with spectacular own-goals only adding to the dishonour of defeat. He became an exile in his own side, left out more often than not, his name only making a rare appearance on the team sheet.

Apparently a nowhere man, left to rot in the reserves

or to be loaned out into obscurity, Friedrich was down but not out. He patiently rebuilt his reputation, playing his way back into the side. His was the story of the comeback king. Again and again he would do it until he made a virtue of the ups and downs of his journey through football. A flash continental in the changing-room even had an expression for it: *déjà vu*; Friedrich just answered: 'Seen it all before, mate.'

And so Friedrich, this most restless of players, always in and out of trouble, with a career plagued by injury, learnt to play his game not only to the full, but for the moment as well. After all was said and done, in Friedrich's book, without footballers there wasn't football. He was unerring in his belief that if his team was to survive in the top flight the players had to be strongly independent in mind and physical presence. A desperate end-of-season scrap for points beckoned the club to the unknown, with goal-difference calculations beyond all but the natural-born programme-collector and match statistician. Standing alone at the heart of the defence, Friedrich knew a heavy responsibility was being laid on his shoulders. Out of the chaos he was determined to find order – one place above the relegation cut-off line would do him just fine. With studs up, his tackle that saved the club's season was a real horror-show. Cynical, but professional, he had done his job: the goal that would have given the other side their certain victory wasn't to be. He hardly bothered to look round as the ref's hand went straight to that fateful pocket from where the card would be drawn. Friedrich knew there was little or no point in protesting, there was only one conceivable colour. And so, with the red card flapping in the podgy little fingers of the proverbial short, fat, balding bastard in the black, Friedrich trotted off for his early shower and bracing rub-down. His career was at an end, this was one tackle too far. In a way Friedrich was relieved. He couldn't stand the hero-worship that would have surely beckoned out on the pitch. Instead, it was in that solitude, alone in the dressing-room, he had found his calling at last, the unfulfilled potential of the little lad with a big motor who could have been a contender for international honours if only he'd listened to reason.

Ludwig Wittgenstein

Cambridge United and Austria
Number 6: Central Defender

'Imagine people amusing themselves in a field by playing with a ball. Throwing the ball aimlessly into the air, chasing one another with the ball. The whole time they are playing and following definite rules. Is there not also the case where we play and make up the rules as we go along?'

LUDWIG WITTGENSTEIN, *Philosophical Investigations*

The enigmatic central defender Ludwig Wittgenstein frustrated many with his darting runs which never seemed to quite end up where he intended. Again and again he would head off upfield in a new direction. Sadly though, he would never quite complete the move with the single telling pass that might have brought the game to a winning conclusion.

The architect of the defence, Ludwig could also on occasion be a brutal disciplinarian. Never very good at conceding defeat, his punishing tackles would send a shiver down the spine of the most courageous of forwards. But it was the structure of the side that worried him most of all. In his early days he sought to build the team around his midfield mentor Bertrand Russell but eventually he found Russell's game wanting. His distribution of the ball was too general, with the result that the game would shift all over the pitch to no obvious effect. Ludwig came to think that possession was the key, giving the side a necessary sense of order.

With his pin-point accurate balls setting the forward-play in motion, Ludwig's slow but patient build-ups soon became a feature of endless TV action-replays. Des, Gary and the dreadlocked Ruud would drool over his passing with the former Liverpool lynchpin Hansen recounting time and time again in his slow Scottish lilt: 'Every picture tells a story.' At first, Ludwig was happy to go along with this *Match of the Day* mythology about how he played the game. After all, it seemed to be the logical way to explain the secrets of his success. But as he added to his tactical repertoire, he came to the conclusion that not every action on the pitch could be so easily portrayed. Life was not a table football, you couldn't always flick and expect to win. Take a banana-kick: this wasn't a device to bombard the opposition goalmouth with a barrowload of Gordon Strachan's favourite fruit, it was a top-spin bender heading surely for the top corner of the goal past the outstretched fingers of a beaten 'keeper's hands. The game that was played out in front of the cameras, then beamed on to our living-room screens, was full of hidden intricacies that mere pictures couldn't depict. The basis of the game remained possession and then accuracy in front of goal – this was a fundamental truth that Ludwig was more than happy enough to accept – but he came to believe that there was not just one way to score but many.

It was through the game that the ball was given a sense of meaning. This was Ludwig's new starting point. Without the game the round spherical leather lump was simply an inanimate object devoid of meaning outside of itself. We could picture it in our mind heading skywards bound for goal, but without the players in intricate formation teasing it across the bobbles and divots of the pitch it remained inert, stationary in the world. The game needed a system, some activity to give it a direction. He would point to the ball and then to his players' feet, and he would coax from them the basic understanding of what it meant to kick. Some never quite learnt and would hoof, humph, lash, anything but kick. They were quickly sold off to ply their trade with the dullard artisans of former Cambridge graduate John Beck's team, or would head off to Ireland and claim strange lines of parental lineage to wear the green of their long-lost homeland. With patience, however, the association between word and object began to pay dividends and the ball would come ricocheting off their highly polished boots with unerring speed.

Next, Ludwig employed the services of the midfield general Goethe. He taught the players the basic theory of colour recognition, and to the simple skill of kicking was added the vital capacity to pass the ball to players of their own side, easily identified by all wearing the same colour shirt. Ludwig was troubled, however, by this apparently simple solution to the question of uniformity. In his youth he had turned his back on his adolescent heroes Manchester City. He had burnt their sky-blue shirt, appalled at the man-made colour combinations that had ruined a decent kit, not to mention the decibel-busting melodies of their celebrity fans Oasis, who offended his more classically attuned ears. Troubled by this memory, he wondered whether this act of wanton destruction had destroyed in him the ability to recognize his current team-mates, who ironically were themselves

kitted out in sky-blue. But it was the object of the merchandising department that he had destroyed, not the essence of sky-blue, and so the chant 'Ludwig Wittgenstein's Sky-Blue Army' could once again make some sort of sense as Cambridge set about their mortal foes Oxford United.

With the passing game now firmly in place, Ludwig whipped out the rule book and sought to teach his young side the basics of a winning team. Joining the team at this time was John Maynard Keynes, who was soon fully employed rushing up and down the wing desperately trying to ensure the forwards had a job to do as they waited for the ball to land at their feet. But Keynes alone couldn't make Ludwig's passes work. It was by learning the rules of the game that the players would be turned into a match-winning combination. The rules gave each individual the reason to commit certain acts. The goal-keeper would use his hands to tip the goalbound ball over the crossbar and be applauded; the hapless defender would brush the ball with his outstretched forearm and a penalty would be awarded. With the crowd cheering their appreciation or crying buckets of tears as the penalty was put away, the rules acquired their sense of legitimacy.

Pictures, games, rules. This was the language that Ludwig spoke, and as the team began to understand his guttural Austrian tones – after all, foreign imports were quite a new feature in those days – a certain mood of satisfaction settled around the previously troubled dressing-room. But Ludwig would never allow his players to relax for a moment. He drove them on, seeking new goals, fresh mountains to climb, more matches to settle. With Johnny-come-latelys like Freddie Ayer preaching the positive virtues of pushing and running towards goal, Ludwig was under pressure to come up with the goods as the match with Ayer's Tottenham Hotspur approached, and sure enough he didn't disappoint.

The team had started to lose touch with reality, lined up across the pitch in so many interconnected positions but no longer reacting to Ludwig's impassioned shouts of command from deep in defence. He needed to give his orders a new sense of meaning as the tide of the game started to turn against him. He demanded goals. Turning his words into actions, he broke forward with a long loping run out to the edge of the pitch. Then, coming back inside, he turned his prophetic call for a goal into an unanswerable swerving ball that left his fans gasping for more. The glory days for Ayer at White Hart Lane came to an end with a bump. Spurs simply had no answer to Wittgenstein's wizardry and Cambridge were the rightful victors. With Tottenham sloping off the pitch, the home fans couldn't even put the shock of defeat into words. It was all too much, Ayer's positivism no match for the flight from reason Spurs' sorry predicament represented.

Ludwig was one of those players always being booked for backchatting the referee. Whether the ball was over the line or not over the line, he knew well enough to be a tautological question to which there could only be one true answer. But when the referee responded with the contradictory 'The goal is neither a goal nor not a goal,' Ludwig knew he was in the doggy-dos. 'Disallowed! Are you effin blind?' he would shout – the goal's reality was plain enough for Wittgenstein alone to see and he reckoned the team had saved the three points with a last-gasp winner. The ref on the other hand was having none of it and the logic was obvious: ball scrapes line, jubilant scorer celebrates goal ready to claim rarely earned win bonus, linesman waves flag to disallow goal, referee brushes away appeals, player gesticulates wildly, mutters something barely audible under his breath, red card shown, player hobbles truculently off the pitch. The failure to determine the difference between the tautology of the appeal and contradicting the ref's fitness to be on the pitch when a dubious decision is made was to be Ludwig's disciplinary downfall. The referees, on the other hand, gloried in their god-given right to verify the goals, tackles and offsides that determined the ebb and flow of the match.

In an ideal game we shouldn't have to depend on such unpredictable goalmouth incidents. The ball should move smoothly up the pitch from one end to the other and across the line to notch up the goals with ruthless efficiency. But all too often, with the wind buffeting around their ears and the sticky mud clawing at the ball skidding across the uneven surface, Ludwig knew his team couldn't force the ball forward if it didn't want to go. He ran on goal from a whole variety of positions, evading lunging tackles by circling the box, encouraging his team-mates to make space for themselves. Occasionally the ball would pop out of a tackle, bounce into the voluminous backside of the other lot's immobile centre-half and trickle over the line. 'Own-goal,' the referee declared. 'What a paradox!' replied the waggish Wittgenstein, grinning ear-to-ear as another ill-deserved victory went Cambridge's way. But with the opposing centre-half still bearing down on Ludwig at a fearful rate of knots, Ludwig's glee was tragically short-lived. Collapsing under a sixteen-stone pile of flailing elbows and knees, Ludwig's delicate frame let out a cry that expressed the pain he felt in a stream of obscenities that turned the air blue.

It was the goal, though, that really mattered. It gave the game a shape, a sense of direction. Through the mist of his bone-jarring pain, Ludwig still held on to that thought as he was stretchered off. He had asked questions of his side, and having put the question, the answer came back: the goal stood and victory was theirs. Each player had found a role and performed it, the team deserved their three points, and, rubbed down with all that embrocation, Ludwig would live to play again. The team now knew what was expected of them: to give their all. Ludwig gave them their orders and they gave of their best in return. In the face of such certainty the result was always going to be a definite, the three points were as good as in the bag.

Oscar Wilde

Bohemians of Dublin and Republic of Ireland
Number 7: Outside-right

'Football is all very well as a game for rough girls,
but it is hardly suitable for delicate boys.'

OSCAR WILDE, *The Epigrams of Oscar Wilde*

Every team needs a flair player, and Oscar Wilde was without doubt a true artist of the ball. Coming out on to the pitch Oscar would take up his position, playing wide, very wide. Cruising up and down the wing, ready to cross into the centre when the fancy took him, his crosses were bent, confusing the defenders with their unpredictable trajectory, never straight but always arched long and high into the box. This was a man who could swing the ball both ways, popping up just where you least expected him.

Oscar was of course a giant amongst men, in almost every imaginable sense. He had absolutely no desire to be ordinary, he was one of those players who stood out in the crowd. Resolutely brave in the tackle, he fully understood the importance of being earnest, while he had the fortitude to rush back into his own half when required to add a spare player to the back four. With the team stretched across the park, he would marshal his fellow players to stonewall those last-minute efforts for an equalizer that his opponents would so desperately seek as the final whistle beckoned. And when his team were receiving a good thrashing Oscar would be one of those who played for pride right to the bitter end of a 5–1 defeat.

Spectacular to look at, his ample girth and loping gait fooled many an opponent. Graceful and elegant for a man of his stature, his balls were exquisite in their delivery as he created moves that ensured the game would be over well before the other side realized the true worth of his talent. A moody player on occasion, his game was all about emotion rather than the huff and puff of movement off the ball. A credit to any side, it was a big surprise to many when his first club offered him a free transfer. Oscar wasn't so shocked, though, for in his experience managers knew the price of everyone, but the value of nobody.

He was one of a trio of Irish exports who liberated the English game from its reliance on pragmatic realism, as exemplified by Charles Dickens, with his Scrooge-like defensive formations, and Kipling, with his gung-ho din about keeping your headers on target when all about you lose the flight of the ball. Oscar was having none of this, and pretty soon, alongside his fellow countrymen George Bernard Shaw, at one and the same time man and superman, and James Joyce, who was a portrait of a young man in defence, Oscar spread the Celtic school of football to the four corners of the land. Selfish on the ball, his skill was for a while doubted by managers who failed to recognize the contribution this unrepentant individualist might make to their side. They confined him to camp, not quite sure if he really was one of them, but with his dazzling runs down the training pitch it wasn't long before he had the coaching-staff convinced and his name duly appeared on the team sheet. Soon enough Oscar was showing the team's tacticians that the unspeakable long ball which went in pursuit of the unmeetable would only leave the big lad up front gasping for air and precious little else. What was needed was Oscar dancing through the tackles, drawing the defenders out of the game and then releasing the ball early, yet too late for the slow-moving defence to recover their shape.

His play was graced with an imagination that made Oscar one of the first great exceptions to the rule that the individualist was a luxury that teams could ill afford. He risked ridicule on occasion and some of his challenges were so gross they were anything but decent. Booked, his convictions simply spurred him on to greater things. One ill-fated manager dubbed him a player of no importance, only to be cruelly punished by Oscar's withering wing-play when his side was drawn against Oscar's in the cup. Oscar was the inspiration behind the team's triumph that day, seeing off his detractors with an effortless performance that belied this most paradoxical of players. He had the talent to turn the fortunes of a game in an instant, yet he couldn't see the sense in surrendering that talent to the demands of others. Some would call this selfish, and it was true that once Oscar had the ball he wasn't a great one for giving up his chances of a goal, but in his defence he'd say he was just elevating fun to the principle of his being. Well, it beats the grim predictability of 'Take each game as it comes', and it certainly had John Motson lost for words anyway.

Keeping his adversaries off-balance, he left them disoriented and confused while he steadfastly refused to conform to the way the game had traditionally been played. A firm favourite with the fans, Oscar's selfishness with the ball, however, meant that he continued to attract more than his fair share of critics too. Eventually he turned their barbed notices on their head. The truly selfish player was the one who expected all eleven of his team-mates to play the same way all season long. In fact, Oscar was genuinely unselfish, because he was for each player doing his own thing. And from this anarchic explosion of unadulterated creativity, Oscar moulded an attacking formation that could take on all-comers. Against well-muscled, fine, upstanding players Oscar favoured a delicate one-touch passing game, full of grace and distinction that soon had these rough-hewn men of brawn running round in circles chasing the game as Oscar masterminded their defeat. A rude picture of health, Oscar maintained a curious attachment to his youth, and long after lesser souls had passed away into retirement he was refusing to concede that he couldn't keep up with the exuberant excesses of players half his age. Consent didn't even come into it.

Throughout his career, he was without doubt a risky player. He would have his off days when nothing seemed to go right. When his ambitions turned on occasion to folly Oscar could be inconsolable, but always he would bounce back, eager to get stuck in once more. In a two-legged cup game Oscar's sides were notoriously difficult to break down. Sometimes they might concede the first leg – that Oscar would pass off as a touch of misfortune – but storming back in the second, he knew that, if they lost again, that would be plain carelessness.

His willingness to risk everything was eventually, however, to be his downfall. Playing under the Queensberry rules, he courted disaster once too often and he was caught out. His lavish play failed him and he was forced to cut inside. Away from the wing the slow-moving game in the packed midfield proved too much. Again and again he tried, but eventually on the third time of asking he was forced to admit defeat. A lucrative signing-on fee from an overseas side seemed a safe option, but Oscar was having none of it. He accepted the transfer

to Reading, knowing that his talent couldn't be locked away for ever, and began to rebuild his career in front of hardly packed houses. The hard labours that he would now face on heavy pitches with the wind and rain lashing across his angular facial features would surely test his resolve. But while others would simply go through the motions, drawing out their long careers for yet one more season, Oscar's play was no mere act. His career, then, was not destined to end in disgrace, for Oscar had established that the pass that dare not speak its name, the one that fools those defences who remain ignorant of its winning ways, would live on. He had liberated the player who wanted to play out wide from those sides who expected to thrive as wingless wonders. He would find a way for countless others to soar up and down the wing, no longer on the outside but inside too.

Denying Oscar the ball was just one way those misguided managers had tried to arrest his progress, but Oscar was superbly gifted at playing with his own side. Knowing how to get the best out of his fellow players, he would tease the ball away from the centre. Released, he would frighten the horses with his galloping charges down the wing. His fleeting moves gave off a sense of speed, when in fact he never broke into anything more than a trot: such was the sharpness of his play that it just felt like you'd never keep up with him. He shook the very foundations of the ground as opponents fled in sheer panic. Shirt lifting in the wind, those long uncontrollable locks sweat-strewn around his ears, Oscar was once more triumphant. Dragging the ball back with his favoured left foot, he sent the defence one way while he went the other. Contrary to expectations Oscar was once more the victor. He had hardly been an industrious player; rather, he would lazily lob an outrageous ball to the near post for a team-mate to poke it home. Oscar stood apart, refusing to accept the playing standards the dug-out tried to impose upon him. He'd cast them an injudicious glance, a shake of his heavy hips and just do his own thing. Frequently impractical, occasionally impossible, his talent was what saw him through the bust-ups that ensued. Oscar was never one to underestimate his own worth to the team – after all, he had once famously declared himself to be a work of art – and his right to express his own individual personality was the single most important clause he would put his pen to in any signing-on ceremony.

Never to earn himself a testimonial from his begrudging peers, Oscar did eventually see out his career on the continent, where his maverick manner went down a storm with those more romantically inclined Latin types. One of the first, too, to discover the appeal of the African game, Oscar remained a true international, never more at home than when putting on a virtuoso performance in some far-off land. The most cynical of body-checks and shoulder-charges might try to put him down, but they couldn't defeat his spirit. Delighting his audiences, he remains an inspirational player to Queens of the South, North, East and West.

Sun Tzu

Forbidden City and China

Number 8: Midfield General

'Know the opponent and know yourself; make one hundred challenges without hazard. Know not the opponent but know yourself; match each victory with defeat. Know not the opponent and know not yourself; court disaster in every challenge.'

SUN TZU, *The Art of War*

Every team needs a midfield general organizing the side's defence, and launching counter-attacks from deep inside their own half. Stocky, running hither and thither, firing on all cylinders, masterminding the defence, unleashing his wingers to catch the other lot's full-backs unawares.

Sun Tzu knew a thing or two about match-winning strategies. He reckoned that with plenty of training, a dose of discipline and some crafty set pieces any side could cause an upset. His was a team, then, of great cup runs, though the long-drawn-out matter of winning the league often proved to be a match too far.

At the heart of his teachings were the five fundamentals. Firstly, *direction.* There was no point little Tzu bellowing out his orders if his players ignored him; they had to want to win, to be joined together in the common fight for three points and the spoils of victory. Secondly, *the elements*. A gale-force wind can turn that short pass into a long, forlorn punt, while a goalie's eyes half-blinded by the sun are hardly going to spot that cracking volley heading for the top corner. Use the elements to your advantage, however, and you'll be 3–0 up before you know it. Thirdly, *circumstances*. Weigh up your chances of victory. Sometimes you need to play the last ten minutes out for a draw and go for the killer-punch in the replay. Fourthly, *leadership*. His captain courageous demeanour combined sage-like wisdom with great ball-control. And finally, *method*. The team had to be properly organized with all sorts of cunning subterfuges at set-pieces which everybody had to learn.

If any of his trusted lieutenants wanted to earn the honour of donning the captain's armband, he had to prove to Sun Tzu his familiarity with the five fundamentals, for, as Tzu put it in his captain's programme notes, 'Those who know will triumph, those who don't will fail.' The managers that ignored Tzu's fundamentals were forced to brave the wrath of their club chairman, and their days were usually numbered.

Ancient Chinese graffiti on walls of the forbidden city: 'Confucius say, Sun Tzu 3, Grasshoppers 0.'

Tzu's followers had the sense of playing a game that matched their side's strengths, which were usually the long ball of route one with a big gangling centre-forward and lots of gut-wrenching craziness in the midfield. The aim was to close down the opposition, refusing to allow them to settle on the ball, breaking up every move before it had even begun and then lobbing the ball deep into the other half. The team weren't lacking in skill, rather they were adapting the game to their particular circumstances, and on the way forcing the world-class footballers they were up against to play the game the way they wanted to play it. They lured them into traps, forcing them to commit themselves early, leaving space at the back. Or they would pretend that they weren't up for the big match, apparently intimidated by those great stadium roars of old, all the time lulling their superstar opponents into a sense of false security.

No time to rest, Tzu's warriors would wage war across the pitch, laying to waste here, snapping at heels there. Dividing the opposition down the middle of the park, the midfield were always poised to attack on the break. A match-winner in Tzu's book had thought through his five fundamentals before attacking, whereas a loser simply didn't bother. With his descendants due to rake it in churning out all those little pocket calculators, it was certainly prescient of Tzu to cast his abacus to the four winds and declare: 'Many calculations mean victory, few calculations mean defeat.' A shirt sponsorship deal with Casio is no doubt in the post.

When preparing for a big cup game – when, as we all know, anything can happen, that's the magic of the cup – Tzu urged his charges to assemble a force equal to the task. Great thinking, Sun old chap: we'd hardly go out of our way to prepare a side unequal to the task, would we? But in the lower reaches of part-time football we

might have to call in a few boys to play in men's boots, or the odd trusty veteran who'd served the club with honour but not much distinction. The key, however you did it, was to pack the side with lads who could run their socks off. Soon the opposition would be reeling, their sharpness blunted, their spirit extinguished, their strength drained and playing resources exhausted. Victory would be Tzu's for the taking.

With a cup run underway, the fire would be stoked in these amateurs' bellies and all those shots of the centre-forward who knocks in goals on a Saturday and knocks in nails Monday to Friday as your friendly neighbourhood chippie would soon be wheeled out to fill in the bits between Gary Lineker's ear-to-ear grins on *Football Focus*. Cup fever sweeps the town and all of a sudden lifelong supporters emerge as if from nowhere.

Tzu carefully moulded his team into winners. The secret of his success is easy enough to learn; it was all about winning without really trying. His strategy was to anticipate what the other team would do and then thwart their every move. If his carefully disguised scouts had failed to suss out their rival's game plan, Tzu offered a second option. When the opposing forwards poured into his team's half he would detail his defenders to man-mark them. Twisting and turning, the forwards would try to shake off their markers but they weren't to be deterred. Robbed of support, unable to make any space for themselves, the forwards failed to create any goal-scoring opportunities.

If this didn't work, Tzu advised making the tackles

early, competing for midfield superiority rather than relying on the back four mopping up the forwards in the box. This meant his midfielders had to play a dual role, winning the ball as well as playing it. The game wasn't exactly pretty, but fired up on passion, it was certainly full of commitment. This was Tzu's least worst option to win the game.

What he avoided at all costs was a frontal assault on the other lot's fortress-like defence. A long-drawn-out siege with balls being lobbed in from every conceivable angle just meant their defence soaking up pressure until the final whistle was blown. This flew in the face of everything Tzu stood for. It lacked cunning and subterfuge, and demanded a huge effort for little reward. His highly mobile forwards, light on their feet and quick-witted, were made for a breaking game, not those six-yard-box confrontations between their back four and our front two.

With his side riding along on the crest of their cup run, the secrets of Tzu's success were soon being mulled over by many an armchair expert. Ch'i was at the core of Tzu's kit bag, full of home-spun training theories.

Never impressed by the body-hugging qualities of Lycra, Sun Tzu's finest always kept their rice-boxes under wraps in training.

This is what gave his side their team spirit, a quality that no cheque book could buy, as Tzu would say as yet another side of overpaid superstars were sent crashing out of the cup. With the Ch'i sorted, Tzu's players would always give their all, united in attack and disciplined in defence. The Tao that he instilled in his forwards meant they had the confidence to play deep, beating the offside trap with a flick of their hips, darting into the penalty area and letting rip with an unstoppable shot before the defenders had had time to think. Their Tao was a matter of always weighing up the options: attack or defend, cross the ball or play down the flank? In making the right choices the forwards would decide the fate of the game.

And when they did, not only was their particular numbered ball sure to be whipped out of the bag and dropped into the mixer for the next round, but the Ch'uan would have been decided. This is the balance of powers that determines defeat and victory. Many would seek it, but few would find Ch'uan until it was too late.

With the balls popping out of the draw, the camera would zoom in on poor Tzu. Was he looking for one of the big boys? No, he would answer, avoiding a strong force is not cowardice but wisdom. The cup for him was all about glory rather than gate receipts, so with the whiff of Wembley in his nostrils he looked for the easy route through to the next round. And when their next opponents were duly announced Tzu took his lads down to the training ground and instructed them in the arts of Hsing that they would need to secure their semi-final place. Four-four-two was his favourite Hsing, though if he thought he needed to fortify the middle ground he'd occasionally experiment with a five-man midfield.

The long march to Wembley ended on a fine May day with his team going down in the little red book of cup history as the greatest giant-killers of them all. Cheng, the sides of orthodoxy, big guns up front and well-organized defences whipped into line by hard-faced managers with a firm hand, had been well and truly stuffed by Tzu's team. For once that well-worn cliché of a bunch of lads you'd be happy to have with you in the trenches was true; warriors one and all, they were full of imagination and surprise, out-flanking the lumbering, well-endowed defences of old by breaking quickly out of their fortress-like defence and playing the ball fast. 'Chinese Take-Away', 'Rice 'n' Easy', the headline-writers had a field day, not even noticing as Tzu slipped away from the victory celebration to retreat into obscurity. The glamour of big-time management wasn't for him, so, using his alias Wu, he disappeared, though when his carefully preserved programme notes were rediscovered centuries later he had managers the length and breadth of here, there and everywhere translating his *Art of War* into those horrible printed-out commands they stick over their desks, like 'Do it Right' or 'Seize the Day', no doubt illustrated with a soppy picture of a panda or a tiger. Ugh! It's enough to make you sick as a parrot.

Umberto Eco

Bologna and Italy

Number 9: Centre-forward

'Football is a ritual in which the disinherited expended their combative energy and sense of revolt, practising spells and enchantments to win from the gods of every possible world the death of the opposing half-back, completely unaware of the establishment, which wanted to keep them in a state of ecstatic enthusiasm, condemned to unreality.'

UMBERTO ECO, *Foucault's Pendulum*

Leading the line in the number nine shirt, Umberto Eco was a player of many parts. Only too aware of his surroundings, he battled with the low, and the high, switching from one wing to the other just like a pendulum, while changing his lines of attack with a bewildering variety of signs that only his side had the knowledge to interpret.

Thrusting forward, he was sometimes so far ahead of his team-mates that he was left up front, all alone, playing a lonely game. But this was by no means his intention, nor his natural inclination. He simply couldn't stand it when others failed to follow, rejecting the way more classically trained players like Theodor Adorno always went outside before playing the ball back in. Umberto preferred to knock the ball about a bit between his fellow front men and came to value this exchange more highly than simply the use any individual put the ball to. In essence, Umberto was a great communicator, spreading the ball around, bringing all eleven players into the game. Dario Fo was one of those who shared Umberto's approach to the game. Accident-prone, Dario found that if you can't play you won't play, so his first-team appearances were few and far between, though when he did perform he always attracted rave reviews.

Umberto liked his fellow-players to keep the game open. He wasn't one to impose order by demanding strict formations. Instead, he preferred to free up the midfield, letting the ball-winners float free as a sign of their liberation from the violent tenacity of their former roles. The means of goal production had changed. The industry of wing-backs rushing this way and that to knock the ball straight up the pitch had changed to cultured balls to feet and intricate passing movements that were positively three-dimensional in shape.

Soon enough the tactics were being translated into points and Umberto's side began to climb the table. But Umberto knew the whole exercise would be academic if these victories weren't turned into trophies and league titles by the end of the season. As results began to go against them – after all, Umberto wasn't the only one who could read the game like a book – he found the need to improvise and adapt the side to the difficult games they knew they had ahead. Roland Barthes was brought in from France to play alongside Umberto up front. Like his Italian colleague Roland liked to signal where and when he wanted the ball, and the new pairing hit it off famously with an uncanny understanding of each other's work. They had their differences, of course, but out of this conflict the two forwards produced much of their best work and soon came to dominate the game for long periods.

Umberto wasn't satisfied, though. He wanted to push the ball wider, further and further out to the very margins of the pitch. For him, there were still too many balls that came straight through the centre. He looked out instead for unexpected angles and it was from these surprise moves that he hoped to really show how far the team had advanced. Umberto's imagination and inventiveness would unlock defence after defence and his goal tally really started to mount up. As a goal-scorer, Umberto

was without doubt the author of his own success, but he also understood the contribution of the structures that were now in place that enabled him to perform this role with such distinction. The team certainly wasn't built around him alone, though right down to the finest detail Umberto ensured that each and every one of them understood the role he expected his players to carry out. If they could grasp that the subject of their game was victory, then he was sure that the goals would follow.

As he delved deep into the personal details of each individual member of his squad, Umberto came to the conclusion that, even though they were all getting on a bit, their middle-age shouldn't hold any fear of physical decline. On the pitch the team gave their all as they cultivated an approach to the game that few could find an answer to. With each goal that Umberto's side scored, the away end was turning into a monastery. The silence was almost deafening. Here was a man who was never likely to lose the plot; instead, he would just stand there at the very heart of things, organizing the characters that would bring the game to another successful ending. For some, Umberto's success was a mystery, for others it was simply thrilling, but all agreed that it was never less than epic.

Umberto shaped his front four into a net-like formation. Running forward with the ball, each player was connected to the other, passing the ball back and forth to great effect. While he was proud enough to wear the number nine shirt and to describe himself as a centre-forward, Umberto insisted that each attack was to have no centre, no inside or outside, but rather it was to be characterized by the forwards' all-round contribution. He adhered to the almost limitless attacking possibilities that he thought his front four could provide him with. In this sense it became remarkably difficult to read a beginning, middle or an end into Umberto's tactics. In the Bundesliga Günter Grass beat a drum for his own version of these tactics, while in South America Gabriel García Márquez ended a near century of trophy-less solitude with a similar playing style. Most famously of all, Thomas Pynchon used Umberto's teachings to create his V-formation that was to dominate the newly reconstituted American club sides from coast to coast.

The escape from any lingering danger of going down was startling, so now Umberto had the breathing-space he needed in order to experiment. He wanted to combine the order of delivering the goals that he knew his side needed, with the disorder that he suspected was required to provide such a certain, and welcome, outcome. Umberto started to instil a more competitive spirit in the side. Every single ball was to be contested to the last, though as a man committed to a clean game he remained singularly unconvinced that blatant provocation would do anything more than bring the wrath of the authorities around his team's heads. The ball-delivery now became more and more haphazard, erratic even, with new American signing Jackson Pollock making an art of popping the ball into the box just where you least expected it. Andy Warhol was another who showed great promise in this role, though he lacked stamina and rarely lasted more than fifteen minutes out on the pitch.

Operating in a forward position, Umberto was now settling the score with some blistering performances. There was still a handful of critics who insisted that he didn't properly understand the game, though few doubted that he took it anything but very seriously. His novel approach undoubtedly did bemuse many. Neither romantic nor heroic, he preferred to find a way that ignored the form book, played around with the configuration, yet he preached commitment and in the end turned out to be nothing less than classic.

Umberto was one who was unafraid to take a stand over the ball, guarding it jealously, yet at the same time he was determined to make it open to all, at least on his own side. When called upon to do so, he could check back quickly too. Involved in the game from back to front, Umberto was booked more than once for dissent, though the accusation never worried him unduly. His dives were, of course, the stuff of legend, and when they earned him a match-winning penalty Umberto would sheepishly admit his enduring faith in fakes. Travelling up and down the pitch he would deliver the ball with precision and great exactness to the feet of his fellow forwards with the expectation that others, apart from himself, could accumulate the goals he knew his side needed to secure their place. His skills were on occasion an illusion, the final delivery letting him down, but Umberto felt this was just one of those things and would hardly harm his image. He wasn't worried by the odd abstract ball that would fly along the reality of the goal-line without actually passing over to notch up the score – after all, the Frenchman Jacques Lacan had made a career out of such impenetrabilities. He detested the lack of purpose and commitment that he knew others still held, knowing that if he was to get in the frame for international contention he could never be detached from the game around him.

Unlike his predecessor, St Thomas Aquinas, Umberto knew that, whilst he had a contribution to make, he didn't have the ability to move heaven and earth. Nor was he an artist in the way of Leonardo da Vinci and Michelangelo, but he did know how to put on an exhibition, and connecting his team's form with their functions he was good enough to fashion a championship-winning side out of their previously unrecognized talents. On occasion they let themselves down, a parody of the team that had put three past Inter Milan the previous Sunday, and Umberto knew that the consistency he craved would be a long time coming; but it was surely on its way. And when they finally did get to lift that long-awaited trophy his team-mates were the first to admit that, when they rose to hold the cup aloft, it was in Umberto's name.

Antonio Gramsci

Cagliari and Italy

Number 10: Inside-left

'Football is a model of individualistic society. It demands initiative, competition and conflict. But it is regulated by the unwritten rule of fair play.'

ANTONIO GRAMSCI, *Avanti!*, 27 August 1918

Antonio Gramsci is the ultimate team tactician, the maverick godfather of seventies Marxism who brightened up many a university common room crammed full with dour followers of the Eintracht Frankfurt School debating the one-dimensional properties of their flat back four.

While others favoured a game of movement, all solid, end-to-end stuff, Gramsci pioneered a game of positional play. He studied the solid walls that defenders erected and the effective way they repelled the most blockbusterish of shots that his thunderthigh forwards could unleash. The great leaps forward were all well and good but as one shot after another came crashing back off the lines of full-backs with their hands delicately poised over their naughty bits, Gramsci decided to try a different approach. They had to detach the defenders from the wall. He infiltrated his players into the box; they would chat aimlessly about their Ferraris, the endless pleasures of the Jacuzzi and their latest page 3 conquests. The defenders were put off their stride, and Gramsci saw the subtlety of his tactics force unexpected holes in the wall from behind the opposition's own lines. Next he learnt to bend the ball sideways, spinning it into unprotected spaces where the defence hadn't expected the ball to pop up as they prepared to guard their goal from a full-frontal assault. The defence crumbled, defeated from within, unable to cope with the breadth of play as shots poured in from every possible quarter.

With his positional play came Gramsci's determined opposition to midfield passivity. The team couldn't sit back when the third goal went in, they had to play to win for the full ninety minutes. And every player would play his part or pretty soon he'd be heading back down the tunnel never to return. 'Out of position' was never a criticism that worried Antonio: he preached the virtues of fluidity, of never being rooted to the spot but moving across the pitch, each player confident in his own ability to lead the line. When the game was going the wrong way, the shouts of 'Sack the board', 'Get yer cheque book out' and so on echoed round the ground, but Gramsci knew the solution was in the players' own hands, or rather boots. Each had to learn to play for one another, gaining allies to their left, right and in the centre. This was football from below, as together they rolled back the score-line and turned ignominious defeat into glorious victory. Passivity meant leaving it all just to the forwards to score and defenders to scramble the ball away. In its place Gramsci preached the virtues of an organic formation, with defenders as ready to tackle back as the back four were to play the ball fast and wide up the wings.

Gramsci's most important tactical innovation, though, was the formation he dubbed Hegemony. The team were going through a sticky patch, the demands of a transitional season had proved too much and Antonio was trying to understand why the club were rooted at the bottom of the table with league-leading ambitions the merest flight of fantastic fancy. He realized that not only was their predicament a result of the referees who punished his breakaway attacks with one undoubtedly short-sighted offside decision after another, but just as importantly the team had got it into their heads that going down was a dead certainty. Thinking of themselves as a bunch of losers, they turned their mindset into reality with defeat after defeat. The strapping centre-half presence of V. I. Lenin stopped the run for a while. With his up and at 'em play he massed the lads on the edge of the penalty box and stormed the Crystal Palace to steal some important away points. But the forward march of his labours finally came to nothing and the forced collectivization of the midfield split the defence down the middle. V'lad done bad, and didn't he know it.

Having found the strong man at the back, Lenin, wanting, Gramsci eyed up a player who promised to give the formation unprecedented breadth by playing far out on the left. Trotsky played to impress but his initial promise of a more flexible attack came to nothing as increasingly his forays into the box proved to be rigid and predictable. While promising the impossible, the goals he actually achieved amounted to a very low tally indeed. Sure enough, when the next team sheet was pinned up, Trotsky's name had been airbrushed out of the picture; exiled to Mexico, he found himself kicking his heels as he waited to be picked.

Neither Trotsky nor Lenin had fully served Gramsci's needs out on the pitch. There were some who continued to champion the case for the man from Tblisi, Joe Stalin. This was a man who wouldn't put up with any opposition and was ready to carve up Europe once the fancy of international competition took him. A brutal disciplinarian, Stalin's Siberian training-camp regime left the players cold, and most definitely not asking for more.

Gramsci instinctively knew Stalin wasn't the man for him, so after a brief scouting mission to Joe's home turf in Moscow, Gramsci returned to the sunnier climes of Italy to try to mould his side into a team of winners a third way, free from a dependency on balls from right, left or even far left. He knew he had a class team but each individual player on his own didn't amount to much: dazzling dribbles ended up going nowhere, long hoofs forward were as likely to go into orbit as land in the six-yard box. An intricate passing game became the new order of play. Playing off each other, the team learnt to co-operate, and with the fans roaring them on from the sidelines, it seemed as though the stadium was one heaving mass willing the ball forwards. And when they came up against a right psycho of a full-back, the players knew that the crafty back pass was a better option than the crunching disappointment of lost possession and broken limbs. The side had a pattern about its play, disorganizing the opposition as they attacked on every conceivable front, a mad dash down the left one moment, the patient passing of the ball across the centre the next.

But class alone wasn't going to win Gramsci the game. He had to find ways to motivate the team apart from their own relationship to the means of goal production. The dull economism of work-rate and percentage football was killing off the team's creative surges, so Gramsci declared for Libero. Each player was to find his own road to goal. Pretty soon, his bargain-basement side was knocking them in like there was no tomorrow against sides which were anything but United. Gramsci was out to prove that the wealth of the moneybagged big clubs wouldn't always guarantee them success.

He involved the whole team. Delicate one-twos brought players into the game rather than left them on long-forgotten sidelines. Gramsci broke down the self-imposed barriers between flair play and the more physical side to the game. Gone were the days of the journeyman footballer, these were players who could read the game inside-out. This approach to football was pasta and vino to Antonio's fans – the old attitudes of knocking the ball aimlessly skywards in the mistaken hope that somebody would be on the end of it to blast it past a hapless 'keeper were no more. With their brains in their boots the side played to feet, an intelligent passing-game that had the whole side working together as a unit.

Running desperately hard to keep up with play, the black-shirted forces of the law tried to rule the game with their coercive use of the whistle. The decisions went against Gramsci's side more than most. After all, his was a team of underdogs trying to topple those who had ruled the league for longer than most could remember. On their own the players knew they couldn't win those vital penalties, so they looked to the supporters to question the referee's parentage from time to time, suggest sexual malpractices and that a diet or an eye test might not go amiss. Separated from the goal-scoring production line and perched high up in the stands, the terrace-borne hordes had a different relation to the game, but their contribution to the final victory became decisive. The fans were civil, a society made up of all sorts but welded together by the common cause. The game they yearned for was cultured, and this was what Gramsci and the rest of the lads out on the pitch gave them in abundance. Full of passion, the passes hit the conjuncture between foot, post and net time and again. As attendances soared Gramsci knew he'd cracked it, by building the broadest possible support for what his team wanted to achieve, turning the league upside-down, putting the bottom clubs at the top, their dream could become a reality.

Disciplined, but never an authoritarian, Gramsci added new dimensions to the way to win a game. But his was a school of the hardest of knocks: sentenced on trumped-up charges, he was destined to spend his most productive years in jail. Yet unlike his fellow players he didn't try to earn a quick buck with an exclusive tabloid tale of life behind bars. Instead, he scribbled down all his jailbound thoughts in his carefully compiled prison notebooks, later smuggled out for his followers to piece together and one day construct into the tactics that

would bear his name. In his writings he never assumed that his side had some special right to win. The chronological determinism of the Tottenham school and their fixation with years that end in the number one was not for him. Nor would simply calling yourself United be enough – the team had to earn that most valuable of monikers. To that end, he championed a flexible approach, combining goal-scoring tactics with a match-winning strategy. Scuttling across the pitch this bespectacled, dwarflike hunchback was amongst the first of the players to be dubbed 'crablike'.

And so, just like fellow crab Ray Wilkins, Gramsci was not exactly destined to be a Spice Boy, but then he was no drab workerist either. He transcended the limitations of those who economized on flair. Unlike those players who preferred the security of their own penalty areas, Antonio enjoyed the mobility of a roving role that took him to every part of the pitch and left those who tried to mark him simply on the left side of the ground all too easily outmanoeuvred. He brought a new order to a team that previously had been hopelessly divided, while injecting a fresh feeling and passionate belief in their own ability. He could knit his brows and gruffly stare at his shoes with the pessimistic best of them as he thought through his post-match analysis for the benefit of the TV cameras, while back on the pitch he would give his all for ninety minutes with the wilful optimism of one who knows the game is going to go his way, one day soon.

Bob Marley
Kingstonian FC and Jamaica
Number 11: Outside-left

'Football is a part of I, keep you out of trouble. Discipline. Mek you run in the morningtime. When you run you clear out your head. The world wake up round you.'

BOB MARLEY, *In His Own Words*

Outside-left Bob Marley liked to play the ball on the grass. No dope out on the wing, he would be climbing high, waiting for the ball to balloon skywards from the back. Then, after controlling it in mid-flight, he'd beat his opponent, before taking it slowly down the left deep into the opposition half before slotting the ball home to the wailing delight of his fans.

Caught in possession, Bob knew how to find his way out of a jam. Get up, stand up, and before you knew it he was on the move again. His hit-rate was prodigious, and it was no surprise when Bob was pretty soon top of the rankings as a goal-scorer. But it was as a provider of those essential goal-assists that he was to become a real legend, and a first choice for any self-respecting fantasy league player. Bob himself preferred natural mysticism to the appeal of fantasy but then that's just a minor anthropological point.

He certainly knew all about his roots. Plenty had failed in their ambition to fill the number eleven shirt. Elvis Presley was the king for some but he was hounded and dogged by persistent, tight-marking defenders, stepping on his highly prized blue suede boots, and he got all shook up. Bob Dylan could rock many a defence but his crosses left much to be desired, with the ball just blowing away in the wind. Mick Jagger showed early promise but his fellow forwards complained they just couldn't get any satisfaction when they asked him to pass the ball instead of making one of those long mazy dribbles that became his trademark.

All of these had certainly had their moments, but Bob played to a different rhythm. Slaving away in the midfield wasn't for him. Young, gifted and black, he looked to Marcus Garvey for his earliest inspiration, and a whole line of black stars who were to be his guiding light, inspiring him on to the very highest reaches of the game.

As his career gathered pace, Bob was a revelation out on the wing, and those who played against him knew

they'd have nothing but dread after he'd run them ragged right through the ninety minutes. With Bob on your side the final victory would surely be yours. He was an independent player, but advocated at the same time that the majority should rule, which, coupled with an inclination to win the ball by any means necessary, saw him in trouble more often than he would have liked. His movement was full of consciousness, and off the ball his clenched fist had a power that was a match for any man. Things really only got out of hand though when one of his blistering shots hit the referee, but when it was claimed the ricochet caught his deputy too, Bob denied all. 'It was in self-defence,' was his honest plea, with the early bath beckoning, and the historic judgment of 'self-defence is no offence' was duly carried.

His attacking system was sound enough, recording hit after hit on the opposition goal. This was a team that initially played in harmony. But his early playing partners failed to keep up with Bob. Peter Tosh in particular got all sensitive about his high tackle and, after being sent off for the umpteenth time in his career, demanded the league authorities legalize it. Bunny Livingstone similarly fell out of favour, declaring that Bob was too soft, and went off wailing on his own when the side lost. Bob wasn't to be put off his stride by these distractions, and with a rushed rearrangement of his attacking options, it wasn't long before he was back putting the goals past every 'keeper who dared to get in his way.

Threatening to riot, Bob's side were so fast they were in danger of catching fire if they weren't careful. He urged his fellow players to simmer down, to play the game at their own pace. When the two number sevens clashed, he urged calm. The referee had to find a way of bringing peace to a game that threatened to get out of control with a hurricane of blows. As the game settled Bob did what he was best at, recording another home win, and the three points were his.

He was an early exponent of the long throw, his arm like a burning spear as he rained the balls in, and up front there was always a big youth to connect and put them away. The league title soon became a possibility, but the side had to keep on moving if they were to keep their slender lead. It was always tough at the top, with the chasing pack only too eager to shoot you down. It was time for the team to liven up, so there was an exodus of the elders, players who'd served the club well but were now too slow for the hectic touring and training schedule.

The team still needed a ball-winner who could mash it up in any contest for the ball, and a quick mover who would rush-release it to Bob himself out on the wing, while others provided the back-up he knew he'd need on the road to victory. Lee Perry proved to be more

Bob steps on the grass, woolly tights and hat an optional winter extra.

than just a scratch player and was soon producing the goods that Bob craved for, hard-fought victories at places where they'd thought they would be lucky to escape with a draw. Bob of course was all for the odd draw, one point was better than none after all. But he knew if they wanted to get as high as possible it was all three points they'd need.

All that cool running down the wing was beginning to pay off, and under the influence of their gifted winger Bob's side were well and truly in the race for the title. Some made the mistake of thinking that Bob was a solo artist, but in fact he was just laying down the tracks for his midfield wing-backs to follow. With each goal the cause for furious celebrations by the entire side, Bob just had one question for his team-mates: 'Is this Love?' Sure, Bob, but not as you know it, son: the people will only be ready for that when you put three past Manchester United on the last day of the season and then you can really satisfy your soul. A few months back this had been a side battling for survival. Now they were truly redeeming themselves, and Bob saw the hand of God in all of this. Quite a few distraught goalkeepers agreed as they saw yet another penalty decision given against them.

To lift the title, though, would, Bob knew, take an almighty effort. And there would be no second coming if they lost out. As judgment day approached there were plenty ready to prophesy the result. But Bob ensured the lads took nothing for granted. There was no point getting all ecstatic, on their uppers, when there was still all to play for.

At the back he knew he could rely upon Marvin Gaye to know what was going on, while Curtis Mayfield would move the ball on up for their very own master blaster, Stevie Wonder, to make best use of any set-piece situations. Scoring goals in open play had been the problem in the last few matches. If his forwards hadn't suffered such a goal famine the number one spot would have been theirs already. So Bob made the bold move of snapping up a transfer-deadline bargain. A Free Nelson Mandela was a better deal than almost anyone else Bob could have imagined to play for him up front. Bob didn't believe this meant that they would now waltz away with the title but there were plenty now who would sanction his side's success. So with the frontline jazzed up by old-timer Miles Davis, Bob looked to see who else should accompany the attack. Jerry Lee Lewis was known to supply great balls but Bob was singularly unconvinced. He needed a supplier who was more in tune, who might feed the ball back when called upon to do so while knowing that at the end of the day the word of his captain, Bob, was gospel. Haile Selassie, the conquering lion of African league title chasers, Ethiopia, was the obvious choice. Bob believed he now had the side to take the title.

But as the minutes ticked away to the end of what was the last game of the season it did look like it wasn't to be their day. That is, until Bob popped up on the wing and broke free from the defender who'd been needling him for the previous eighty-nine minutes. Equality wasn't in it as he jammed his way between the two full-backs who blocked his path, and scored the deciding goal. Bob had finally made it. They were dubbed 'the Champions', the number one spot was his, at last.

CAMUS
1

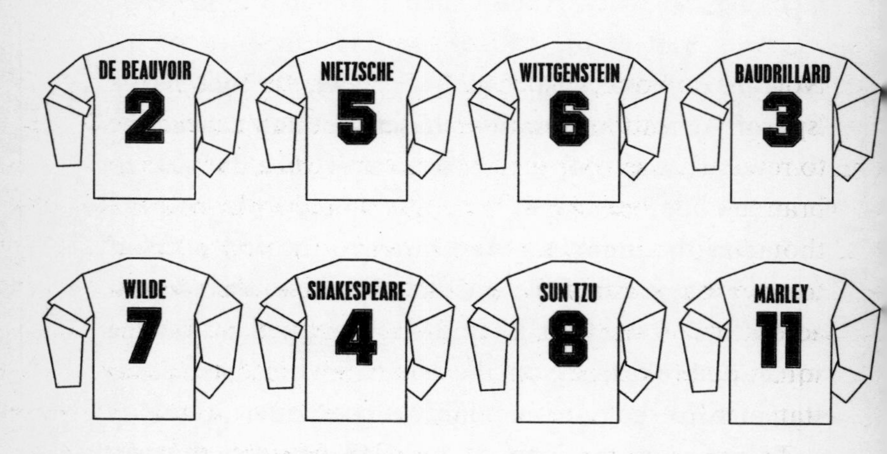
DE BEAUVOIR
2
NIETZSCHE
5
WITTGENSTEIN
6
BAUDRILLARD
3
WILDE
7
SHAKESPEARE
4
SUN TZU
8
MARLEY
11

ECO
9
GRAMSCI
10

Index

Picture Credits

Albert Camus © Harlingue/Viollet.
Albert Camus and his football team in Algiers *c.* 1930 © Collection Viollet.
Simone de Beauvoir © Archive Photos.
William Shakespeare © Collection Viollet.
Football as played in sixteenth century, engraving by Crispin de Passe © Mary Evans Picture Library.
Sun Tzu, based on a thousand-year-old wood-block portrait.
Football as played in China, wood-block engraving from *Sancai tuhui* encyclopedia, 1607, 15024.a.1, © the British Library.
Chinese characters representing 'football'.
Antonio Gramsci © Collection Viollet.
Bob Marley © Kate Simon/Sygma.
Bob Marley playing football © A. Boot/Camera Press.
Jean Baudrillard © M. Dupuis.
Friedrich Nietzsche © AKG London.
Oscar Wilde © Corbis-Bettmann.
Umberto Eco © Mike Powell/Camera Press.
Ludwig Wittgenstein © AKG London.